GOLDEN NUGGETS OF TRUTH

Christian Wisdom for Church Life and Mission

Barry L. Callen, Ed.
with Kevin W. Mannoia and
Don Thorsen

EMETH PRESS
www.emethpress.com

GOLDEN NUGGETS OF TRUTH: CHRISTIAN WISDOM FOR CHURCH LIFE AND MISSION

Copyright © 2024 by Barry L. Callen, Kevin Mannoia, and Don Thorsen
Printed in the United States of America on acid-free paper

All rights reserved. No part of this book may be reproduced or transmitted in any form or by any means, electronic or mechan-ical, including photocopying, recording, or by any information storage and retrieval system, without the written permission of the publisher, except where permitted by law. For permission to reproduce any part or form of the text, contact the publisher, Emeth Press LLC, P. O. Box 533, Jackson, Georgia 30233, www.emethpress.com.

Library of Congress Cataloging-in-Publication Data

Names: Callen, Barry L.;Thorsen, Don; Kevin Mannoiaeditor in chief.
Title: Golden nuggets of truth : Christian wisdom for church life and mission / [by Barry L. Callen].
Description: Jackson, Georgia : Emeth Press, [2024] | Summary: "Barry Callen, Kevin Mannoia, and Don Thorsen share their best thoughts about the Christian faith in today's world. They intend to instruct and inspire young disciples of Jesus, and maybe shake up a few older ones who have fallen asleep. These are golden nuggets of Christian truth, eternal wisdom from past ages that are very much for today. These pages are not a book of quotes. It's more an urgent agenda of priorities for today's church"-- Provided by publisher.
Identifiers: LCCN 2024005041 (print) | LCCN 2024005042 (ebook) | ISBN 9781609472030 (paperback ; acid-free paper) | ISBN 9781609472047 (kindle edition)
Subjects: LCSH: Systematic theology; doctrines. | Christian life-
Classification: LCC BX7027 .C36 2024 (print) | LCC BX7027 (ebook) | DDC 289/.9--dc23/eng/20240228
LC record available at https://lccn.loc.gov/2024005041
LC ebook record available at https://lccn.loc.gov/2024005042

The Garden, The City, and The Journey

In the midst of our life journeys, we now-fallen humans are able to look back and ahead. We have a distant memory of the Garden of God where once we were dressed in splendor, our robes studded with jewels. The onyx, jasper, sapphire, and emeralds were all in settings of engraved gold. We beloved children of God strolled in magnificence (Ezek. 28). Then things went very wrong.

The Bible also provides a glimpse of the City of God that yet might be ahead somewhere beyond our fallenness. It will shimmer like a precious gem. An angel guide already has measured the City with a golden rod. The gates are pearls and the walls garnished with every precious gem imaginable (Rev. 21). As in the original Garden, all sparkles with reflections of the Divine and we again will be privileged to stroll in a renewed magnificance.

"God's Word is a lamp for our feet and a light for out paths" (Ps. 119:105). "Even though I walk through the valley of the shadow of death, I will fear no evil, for you are with me, your rod and your staff they comfort me" (Ps. 23:4). "Faith is the assurance of things hoped for, the conviction of things not seen" (Heb. 11:1). "So we do not lose heart. Even though our outer nature is wasting away, our inner nature is being renewed day by day. . . We look not at what can be seen but what cannot be seen, for what can be seen is temporary, but what cannot be seen is eternal" (2 Cor. 4:16-18).

Our long human journey between the gleaming Garden and the radiant City is an upward path of faith. The Bible graciously provides numerous signposts to assist. Our fallenness must be resolved before our glorious destination is gained. These pages are filled with samples of "golden nuggets" of needed traveling wisdom for our faith journey. They are central and dependable Christian perspectives on the nature of God, the Son, the Bible, the church, and the faith journey and its destination.

"Much like the popular 20th-century publication *Leaves of Gold*, *Golden Nuggets* promises to become a popular devotional companion for Christians. Featuring a wide variety of prominent authors, it offers inspirational and thought-provoking quotes on key Wesleyan-Holiness theological themes. This book is a perfect gift for both laity and ministers!"

--Dr. Cheryl Bridges Johns
  Distinguished Visiting Professor
  & Director of Pentecostal House of Study
  United Theological Seminary

Contents

	Pages
Preface……………………............................	ix
I. The God Who Really Is…………………….........	2
II. The Son Who Fully Embodies………………….........	20
III. The Book that Properly Records……………........	38
IV. The Thought that Helpfully Conveys…….............	54
V. The Experience that Truly Transforms…................	78
VI. The Community that Faithfully Serves.................	96
VII. The Spirit Life that Boldly Empowers.................	116
VIII. The Hope that Deeply Assures……………….....	136
Contributors………………………….......................	153

Barry L. Callen

Don Thorsen

Kevin W. Mannoia

We three Christian colleagues and many others (names listed at the end) have deep appreciation for the Christian faith and its relevance for the personal and social needs of our time. In these pages we seek to identify "Golden Nuggets" of truth, brief pieces of enduring Christian wisdom on which believers today can build and rely, and to which they can testify with their words and lives. May God speak to you as together we hear carefully, obey faithfully, and witness with joy.

Preface

We are community together in Christ. Found here for the good of the whole body are the best thoughts of many church leaders developed over decades of study and serving. The thoughts are about all key aspects of the Christian faith as it is rooted in biblical revelation, centered in Jesus Christ, and particularly relevant to today's world. We hope to instruct and inspire young disciples of Jesus, and maybe shake up a few older ones who've fallen asleep.

These concise perspectives we're calling "golden nuggets" of Christian truth. For your convenience, they are small units of wisdom, easily read and immediately useful for private devotion, group discussion, or sermon preparation and other forms of public testimony. Don't think of these pages as a collection of quotations from a large number of particularly prominent Christian writers, although they certainly are that. They also form an urgent agenda of priorities for today's church.

Essential Building Materials

We are not acting here as systematic theologians presenting finished truth statements pre-organized into some large body of mandatory belief. We are not functioning as theological architects designing in detail how the house of Christian truth is to be built, including all its internal arrangements and final external appearance. Those tasks require large books of detailed theology structured around given personalities or themes or modern thought fads. Such is not our task here.

We are theological educators and discipleship mentors in a testimonial mode on behalf of the church's contemporary life. We aren't functioning as theorists and speculators with an experimental and innovative agenda. Our intent is to bring forward the best of the Christian past, golden nuggets judged to fit for any time, and especially appropriate for our current culture to which we hope to bear a Christian witness.

We're doing what we see happening in the Bible itself. It does not present a finished systematic theology. Its many reports and beliefs are presented in multiple languages and cultures and developed over centuries of time. Biblical "theology" is always under construction. There are fundamental nuggets of truth seen throughout the sixty-six "books" of Scripture. They are essential regardless of shifting times and thinkers, styles and emphases, worship patterns and religious structures that always are in motion.

Our present effort comes prior to any detailed theological blueprints and is broader than any given denominational structure. We are looking for the essentials that transcend such particulars and variations and groupings. Envision with us a building constructed of Christian truths to house and nurture today's Christian life and mission. Found here isn't the highly designed plan of construction. Instead, we are previewing a simple structure with eight floors of thought and belief. Each is understood to be essential for any time or place in the teaching and witnessing journey of the church of Jesus.

Each of these eight floors (book chapters) lacks an exact layout plan and infrastructure. What we have placed on each floor are only key building blocks, essentials, golden nuggets of enduring Christian truth, biblical basics that always should be found and treasured. Christians have and will name and decorate and arrange these differently. This diversity should be of little concern as long as the golden nuggets are clearly present. Jesus warned about building on sand rather solid rock.

Even When in a Hurry

Today's secular culture, and maybe even the church, is encouraging people to focus quickly on less and less, one click, a glance, a commercial of fifteen seconds, the flash of an image or two, upbeat music that speeds up everything. For those now in that mental mode, these golden nuggets of Christian truth get right to the point in as few words as possible. We've gone back through our many past published materials and checked with the work of our wise Christian friends. We've spotted pivotal truths that can stand alone, minus all the previous documentation. They follow as essential fixtures and furniture for each floor of the structure of Christian truth.

The truth structure is always under construction, but we hope never with shoddy materials. We won't tell you how to position the nuggets of essential furniture in each room or label and paint them for prime appearance. Diversity always will exist. That's an enrichment we should learn to enjoy and not fear.

These golden nuggets are thought starters for church discussion groups, flashes of wisdom to light patches of our surrounding darkness. They are sermon launchers if you are a pastor, and quick nudges from God for any believer or occasion. There's no shallow froth here, only serious substance presented in relatively few and non-technical words. Our task is to enrich, not endanger, and clarify, not confuse.

Do you have a free moment in the car while stuck in traffic or in a crowded room waiting for the doctor who never seems to come? Need a spiritual jolt to launch the morning or a warm assurance of truth as sleep nears at night? Need help in evaluating how your church is doing, maybe a priority agenda for what it should be doing? Want a thoughtful gift for a friend who doesn't read much but needs at least glimpses of basic Christian truths? A long attention span isn't required, just an open heart and a free moment.

God keeps coming as that still small voice. Are we listening? Paul tells us to pray always. The psalmist tells us to meditate on God's Word at all times. These biblical instructions seem impossible in the crazy rush of our present world. Or maybe they aren't. Meditation can begin with a momentary thought that stimulates. Prayer can be inspired by awareness of a brief truth that turns eyes upward, even if only for a moment. Here are eight floors (chapters) of the Christian house of truth. You are welcome to visit whenever you wish.

God Seeks Your Attention

Real life is much like what we find in the Bible. If you want a fully developed "systematic" theology, you'll look in vain between Genesis and Revelation, or in these pages. Search the Bible and mostly you will find historical reports, little stories, short letters, testimonies, songs of praise, cries for help, quaint parables, and pieces of advice in desperate situations. They come from many voices in many times and places. Paul's book of Romans is a bit of an exception but hard to follow for many modern readers. It was his theology in the making, usually done on the run in response to the situations he was facing.

The truth is all there in the Bible, but presented in bits and pieces more than in long theological discourses or finished creedal statements or fixed religious structures that we should be trying to duplicate today. These pages feature the bits and pieces of Christian wisdom organized by broad themes--chapters. They are essential building blocks for today's church. We are a few current apostles of Jesus doing our best to share the essentials, not the incidentals.

Each golden nugget we share is identified by original author and published work. Consult these fine sources as you have time and interest. If you haven't the time or interest, never mind. At least allow the basic truths to impact how you think and act and serve, maybe even who you are.

God calls for our full attention, if only for occasional moments of our time. Here's a ready reference to our many thoughts over the years. Remember at least this. Christian belief is not limited to an understanding of some extensive systematic theology grasped by the mind. Nor is it merely some classic creed repeated routinely with the mouth. It's allowing the whole of life to be directed by the conviction that certain things Jesus taught about God, humans, salvation, the church, the world, and the future *are actually true,* and thus should be life-changing for us.

These central teachings are what's found here. They include the momentous claim that the Teacher, Jesus, *is the truth!* Being related to him is to be your finest self on the way to your intended destiny.

Gratitude

Words of grateful acknowledgment are in order. This book was greatly enriched by Kevin Mannoia and Don Thorsen joining me on this journey. Soon joining us was a crowd of our wisest Christian friends. We and now you are in their debt. One of them observes this:

> Theologians do not merely amplify, refine, defend, and deliver to the next generation a timeless, fixed orthodoxy. Rather, by speaking from within the community of faith, they seek to describe the act of faith, the God toward whom faith is directed, and the implications of the faith commitment for a specific historical and cultural context. (Stanley J. Grenz, *Theology for the Community of God*).

That's us. We now have joined to bring you not a "fixed and timeless orthodoxy" but a collection of enduring golden nuggets of Christian truth needing to be freshly stated and arranged for this generation and its cultural context. We aren't finishing for you the theological building for today. We're suggesting only the structural framework and a few of the essential fixtures and pieces of furniture that we judge necessary and best. May God guide as you consider these and build from there.

Gratitude also flows from the three of us to Azusa Pacific University for a generous grant in support of this publishing effort. We so appreciate Christian institutions of higher education that actively encourage the pursuit of wisdom both on and well beyond their campuses. God bless Christian higher education!

Your Life and Faith Traveling Companions,
Barry L. Callen, Kevin W. Mannoia, Don Thorsen,
and a community of others.

Often what we need aren't answers so much as an unmovable Rock on which to stand while questions remain unanswered.

> We have an Anchor that keeps the soul,
> Steadfast and sure, while the billows roll,
> Fastened to the Rock which cannot move,
> Grounded firm and deep in the Savior's love.
>
> "Will Your Anchor Hold
> in the Storms of Life?"
> (Priscilla J. Owens)

The Truths of God
For the People of God

For as the heavens are higher than the Earth, so are my ways higher than your ways, and my thoughts than your thoughts. . . . The LORD is gracious and righteous; our God is full of compassion. (Isaiah 55:8; Ps. 116:5)

We look not at what can be seen, but at what cannot be seen, for what can be seen is temporary, but what cannot be seen is eternal. . . . Hear, Israel: the Lord our God, the Lord is one. Love the Lord your God. (2 Cor. 4:18; Deut. 6:4-5)

I

The God Who Really Is

Here is where everything theological begins. This is the ground floor of the house of truth. Get right your views about God and you will be ready to think and act properly about everything else involved in the Christian faith. How sad that we are tempted to believe almost anything but the truth about the real God.

Following are twenty-one golden nuggets of Christian truth that illumine the problems and possibilities of coming to know and love and be changed by the one real God known through biblical revelation. They begin with a few nuggets that reveal our necessary ignorance at how God sometimes works in this troubled world. Often our beliefs must be tinted with caution, humility, and patience. Only in Jesus Christ does the fullness of divine revelation reside.

Glimpses of the following Golden Nuggets

1. The real God surely couldn't be known unless wanting to be.
2. Faith may be a stretch, but not a blind leap.
3. Human freedom is a choice of divine love.
4. Do we dare even write or speak aloud the name of God?
5. Have you been disappointed with God's performance?
6. Why would anyone worship a "god" with no brains?
7. Does God suffer Attention Deficit Hyperactive Disorder?
8. Was God really guilty of what happened at Auschwitz?
9. What or Who controls events, God or our power politics?
10. Are we human ventriloquists stupidly trying to talk for God?
11. Nothing is impossible with the real God.

12. The biblical God cannot be contained or controlled.
13. The God who once was, still is, and always will be.
14. A 'Trinity" is so true of the one real God.
15. Is God really a man? Then where does that leave women?
16. The cross of Jesus means that God is known best in pain.
17. Is TULIP or ROSE God's best flower?
18. God seems to have three somewhat different wills.
19. The God of power doesn't prefer over-powering humans.
20. Jesus' parable of the prodigal son is about the real God!
21. The real God works in ways that sometimes make us laugh.

1. THE REAL GOD OF THE BIBLE

The Bible tells the story of God with us in Israel and now in Jesus Christ. God would be unknowable by us mere humans unless God chose to be known. Biblical revelation tells us that God has chosen to be known, particularly in three special ways. God initiates conversation and calls us to *communion*. God comes to where we are and calls us to *faith*. God takes us by surprise and calls us to *mission*. It was the incarnation of God in Jesus that was the ultimate divine surprise. It's when the supreme divine mission of today's church was launched.

The God of the Bible is the eternal missionary who comes to where we are to establish the kingdom of heaven and incorporate us into the ongoing missionary venture. This is a radically different kind of deity than typically found in either religious or philosophic history. In those places the divine often is pictured as either as humans blown large or as a stupendous mystery disconnected from the daily circumstances of our lives. The God of the Bible is neither of these. Instead God, although categorically different from us, nevertheless has become one with us by revealing definitively his true identity and purpose in Jesus Christ, and by inviting us to join him on mission through the presence and gifting of the divine Spirit.
–Gilbert W. Stafford, *Theology for Disciples*

2. FAITH NO BLIND LEAP

Belief in God is not a "blind leap" of faith. Such supposed blindness is inaccurately associated with Danish theologian Søren Kierkegaard who described faith as a "leap of faith." He meant by leap a passionate, existential trust in God who is intensely personal. But this faith leap is hardly blind, ignorant, or unfounded. Medieval Christians talked about faith as having three components: knowledge, assent, and trust. Christians have *knowledge* about Jesus. They *assent* to the knowledge they have about the life, death, and resurrection of Jesus, and then they *entrust* their lives to the person and gospel of Jesus.

There is no blindness involved in entrusting oneself to that which one has freely assented on the basis of received and trusted knowledge. Christians believe that biblical claims about God as Creator and Savior are as reasonable as alternative worldviews. This belief does not prove the truth of the biblical perspectives, but it does make clear that Christian faith is reasonable faith, not blind, unfounded, or simplistic. The faith is in God the Father known by faith as *Abba*, that is, God known in the most personally intimate, positive, and supportive of ways. –Don Thorsen, *What's True about Christianity?*

3. FREEDOM AN EXPRESSION OF LOVE

There is an important distinction to be made between "belief" and "hope." I hope no one suffers in eternity for refusing to humble themselves, repent, and believe in Jesus as Savior and Lord. I believe there is sufficient biblical evidence to encourage expecting that God will give people many chances to be saved. Likewise, I believe there is sufficient biblical evidence to encourage the viewpoint that not everyone will accept God's saving grace—past, present, or future. It's the risk God has taken, so to speak, in creating people with a real freedom of choice.

Because God is love, it was important that God give people freedom to choose, to accept or reject the good news in Jesus Christ, to accept or reject God's love, to accept or reject eternal life. It's like parents giving birth to children, knowing that as their babies grow older, they may love their parents or not. Although human analogies break down when trying to describe God, they at least give us a hint of the great love of God in making the choice to grant us freedom. –Don Thorsen, *What's True about Christianity?*

4. LOST IN MYSTERY, FOUND IN HISTORY

The very name of God was so sacred in the Jewish tradition that care had to be taken when daring to speak it aloud or even touch it once written. One of the Ten Commandments focuses on not taking the divine name "in vain." This was more than blasphemy. It included representing God's name in an unworthy manner. "God" has been known by many names across cultures and centuries and religious traditions. Some, likely most, suggest something that God is not, or at least affirms less than all God really is.

Picture theologian Paul Tillich sitting on a beach staring at the ocean with tears streaming down his cheeks. He tended to avoid using the word "God" in his theological books. Why? To him God is hardly another being alongside all of us beings. He preferred "Ground of Being," the originator and base of all beings. Gazing at the ocean, Paul was overwhelmed by the unimaginable immensity and inexpressible mystery, and yet a vastness as close as the sea breeze in his nostrils. It seemed loaded with a revealing and relating love. God is not left without self-witness in our real human history. The unknowable wishes to be known and have life-changing relationships with us human beings! This divine self-revealing has a name, Jesus. –Frederick Buechner, *Beyond Words*

5. IS GOD A DISAPPOINTMENT?

God is a great disappointment to many people. God fails to answer all our questions, lets tyrants succeed, and allows us humans to make self-destructive choices. "Conservative" believers are anxious for God to smite sinners with deserved judgment, which often doesn't happen, at least not in this world. "Liberals" reject classic teaching about God because of evil being allowed to run rampant, which doesn't seem to fit their logic of who God should be. God becomes for them only a symbol of their own best ideals. We all struggle with the clash between a supposedly powerful and perfect God of love and a badly broken creation.

The Bible reveals a God who offers freedom to us humans, allows the possibility of evil, and also is poised to triumph eventually against all contrary forces. It's natural to fear the great Enforcer. It's so wonderful to have opportunity to be graciously related to the great Lover! Atheism in part is an unpaid bill of the church which too often has presented God as remote and unsympathetic and existing at humanity's expense. Faith too often puts a damper on the good life. Often atheists refuse to believe because they have not been told about the real God of the Christian gospel who loves us freely, wants a joyous relationship with us, and is anxious to empower us for the best we were created to be. –Clark H. Pinnock, *Most Moved Mover*

6. WORSHIP "GODS" WITHOUT BRAINS?

It's a troubling story that shows deities without brains, gods without guts, an idol shop without inventory, and humans desperately trying to save their own divine creations. It's a Jewish legend about Abraham, father of the faith. When a kid, he was in his father's idol shop. A man came to buy and Abe blew the sale by asking, "Why would a mature person like yourself buy and worship an idol made here only yesterday by my father, one without even a tiny brain?" According to the prophet Isaiah, Babylon once was parading its beloved idols, intimidating its Jewish captives. Things went crazy along the parade route. A camel tripped and its idol-carrying float flew into the ditch. A nearby elephant lurched and its poor god smashed to pieces.

We worship our own greed, drool over favorite sports teams with the most wins and politicians with the most pull, preachers with the biggest congregations and nations with the biggest bombs and latest satellites. We buy in shops with the newest shiny idols even when knowing they lack brains (Jn. 2:16). Could young Abe talk you out of buying an idol? They sell out in a hurry! The *Devil's Dictionary* defines "Olympian" as relating to a mountain in Thessaly once inhabited by gods, but now the repository of yellowing newspapers, beer bottles, and mutilated sardine cans, attesting the presence of the tourist and his appetite." –Barry L. Callen, *Bible Stories for Strong Stomachs*

7. A CASE OF RELIGIOUS NEUROSIS?

The atheist understandably criticizes any popular "god" claimed to meet all human needs, solve all problems, and satisfy all desires. It's proper to critique the human tendency to religious neurosis of wish fantasy. Biblically speaking, God is not a cosmic bellhop for whom we can press a button to get things done. The prominent biblical stress on divine judgment and call for believers to be self-sacrificing address the atheist's criticism directly. Whatever passes for "popular" religion is hardly the Christian heritage of belief. The psalmist was tempted to fear that God suffered from ADHD (attention deficit hyperactive disorder).

The psalmist threw this prayer at God. "Please pay attention!" (Ps 5:1). God had been hyperactive in the past, creating worlds, people, routing enemies, etc. Now the psalmist was in trouble and no help was coming. Divine ears were deaf and the powerful hands inactive. What we believe and what we see happening sometimes conflict. We are caught between Psalm 8 and 13. We marvel at God's amazing creation and ask, "Why even bother with us?" (8:4). Then we suffer because of divine silence and complain, "Long enough, God, you've ignored me long enough! (13: 1). Is God on new meds? According to a Yiddish proverb: "God will provide, but oh that he would until he finally does!" –Barry L. Callen, *Discerning the Divine* and *The Jagged Journey*

8. WAS GOD REALLY GUILTY?

It's reported that in Auschwitz a group of Jews put God on trial. The awful evil in this Nazi death camp seemed to make all easy answers worse than obscene. The verdict was that God was guilty, either of not being, not caring enough, or at least impotent and unable to stop this terrible circumstance. Other Jews in the camp continued their traditional prayers, still hoping and believing in spite of the appearance of God's terrible guilt. Faith is possible although difficult in the midst of extreme evil. Negro spirituals are "songs in the night," defiant faith in the face of a degrading slavery. What responsibility do wayward humans have? Is guilt wrongly placed on God? Surely God never wills suffering on his children. Then why let it go on? –Elie Wiesel, *Night*

A fallen world generates pain. The coming of the kingdom of God is meant to end the constant presence of disease and pain. When they come, rather than looking for someone, even God, to blame, we are to do our best to ensure that they do not remain unchallenged. We are to pray, yes, but prayer is not a labor-saving device. In the divine presence, we must fall silent before the One beyond our speech ability and speak to others about that One concerning whom we cannot be silent. Jürgen Moltmann was a young Nazi soldier, soon an Allied prisoner of war who saw his homeland bombed to bits. He survived and pioneered the Christian tradition known as the "theology of hope." –Jürgen Moltmann, *The Living God and the Fullness of Life*

9. PROVIDENCE OR POLITICS?

Who or what really controls world events? Jesus came back to Nazareth. What did his hometown people see? Only a local kid showing off after abandoning a widowed mother and impoverished siblings? Can we see the truth when it's standing in front of us? So much goes on behind the scenes. The holy life is guided by an often unseen holy hand. Christian holiness is embracing God's invisible guidance (Psalms 85; Isaiah 30). Who's in charge of events? Sometimes it seems like no one. Now, however, the "mystery of Christ" is revealed by apostles and prophets through the Spirit of God (Eph. 3:4-5).

The deepest of God's intentions are at work even if often out of the sight. The full reality of what is real involves both foreground and background. Realizing that there is an eternal background to world events is what gives meaning and hope to this strange and often chaotic life of ours. Says Paul, "We look not at what can be seen, but at what cannot be seen, for what can be seen is temporary, but what cannot be seen is eternal" (2 Cor. 4:18). We can at least glimpse by faith what for now is largely out of sight. It's God quietly at work. In Jesus, time and eternity were fused. He saw the whole of what was happening, foreground and background. He belonged perfectly to both worlds. To realize this and live in its light is to be holy as God is holy. –Barry L. Callen, *Christian Holiness*

10. WHOSE DOING ALL THE TALKING?

A tabloid headline reads, "Ventriloquist in Coma, Dummy Still Talking!" God, according to some, has fallen gravely ill or even has died, while many of his people go on talking about him, often claiming *for him*. Has God survived the intellectual challenges of modern times or quietly expired under the weight of our expanding technology and communication prowess? Is God still speaking or is it just us stubborn believers still talking constantly, using the divine name in vain in our many theological sentences? Is the heavenly

Ventriloquist deceased while his dummies go on and on about him? Will we ever shut up? If we did, we might again, in pure awe, be in touch with the Holy One who stands beyond our understanding and wishes to speak above our speaking.

God wants to be understood and has provided an avenue for that in Jesus Christ, the Son. Holiness is the key point of contact. God's eternal nature touches us, allowing us to regain our original natures through being reformed into the image of Christ. Willful sin caused estrangement, with the resulting absence of holiness. With a decision of the will, humans may again experience proximity to God through Jesus, resulting in a transformation into being holy as God is holy. Only then does indepth spiritual knowledge emerge. Then God again can speak redemption to the world *through us*. –Kevin W. Mannoia, *Dictionary of Christian Spirituality*

11. IS THE IMPOSSIBLE POSSIBLE?

The "evangelical" movement of Christians is a positive force of God in today's divine work in the world. It cannot be defined precisely and should not be ignored or minimized. Those who try to codify, organize, control or in any way manipulate it as a whole do so at their own peril. Sometimes this contemporary movement of Christians, particularly in the United States, does have a fortress mentality that leads to an enclave of exclusivism. Can this problem be overcome by the God who is committed to inclusiveness? Since God really is, the impossible always can be possible!

The future community of God's people should be characterized by relationships, established through networks, described experientially, celebrated in diversity, driven by mission, and centered on Jesus Christ. The obstacles to this ever happening do seem insurmountable. That's the joy of it! It is impossible for us, but not for God. Our God is not ordered according to our patterns or contained by our structures. In God there is energy that surpasses our ability to confine. In that glorious reality there always is hope. –Kevin W. Mannoia, in Ecumenical Directions in the United States Today

12. CONTAIN THE UNCONTAINABLE?

Reductionism is everybody's problem when it comes to God. "Conservatives" tend to reduce their understanding of God to the boxes of their own limited creeds, spiritual experiences, private understandings, and social agendas. "Liberals" sometimes reduce God to a poetic expression of their own social ideals. None of us should create God in our own image, although we all are tempted to do it, even if unintentionally. The classic book by J. B. Phillips, *Your God Is Too Small!*, is our wake-up call. When we think we know it all, we don't know much. When we aren't sure we know anything, we've lost the anchor of our faith altogether. We are to be patient and cautious, and yet dare to believe! When it comes to God, even when we think big, our thinking will be inadequate.

Who deserves worship today? The arrogant Caesars, the swaggering Genghis Khans, the fearsome Alexander the Greats? These had their brief times before becoming dust in their graves. The Ghandis, Kings, and Lincolns may deserve high respect, but well below the level of worship. We are told, "Blessed are the meek for they shall inherit the Earth." Meekness is not weakness, but self-control under pressure. Look to Jesus who was meek, born a king who left his palace to dwell among common folk like you and me. He was murdered on a cross and stuck in a grave, futile efforts to *contain the uncontainable*. His Father is where worship belongs.
–Barry L. Callen, *The Heart of the Matter*

13. THE GOD WHO WAS, IS, AND EVER WILL BE

The Christian *Trinity* doctrine is not a perplexing numbers game. It's basic Christian teaching with continuing significance for practical life today. The Triune life of God is a relating and sharing life. Instead of belonging to God alone, it naturally is shared with us humans *in the face of Christ* and *in the activity of the Holy Spirit*. We should recognize and celebrate God's life *with us* and potentially *through us* for others. There is no polytheism here (three gods), just the one God, the Father with us in the life, death, and resurrection of

Jesus, and now remaining with us in the Spirit of Jesus, and hopefully through us on behalf of others.

The biblical bookends are revealing. Genesis reports God in the sovereign act of creating. There was no need to do this other than that love tends to reach, share, embrace. Revelation pictures the end of the creation and a new creation. Is life now concluding? Since love never ends, God is pictured as still reaching and inviting. God is in the act of inviting all who wish to take the water of life as a gift. The God who *was* remains the God who *is* and, after the end, the God who still *will be* (although God doesn't inhabit time but invents time!). In the meantime, through the sanctifying and sustaining ministry of the Spirit, God now is graciously active among us, sharing eternal life and assured divine destiny. Shall we invest our lives in what quickly passes away or in what eternally endures? –Barry L. Callen, *Discerning the Divine*

14. THE SINGULAR ONE WHO IS TRIUNE

It's important enough that we speak again of the divine "Trinity." God is not an all-determining, controlling, and detached monarch. Rather, God is a relational and loving Parent who chooses to be genuinely related to this world. Though sovereign and holy, God allows the divine being to be touched by the world, often suffering because of the world (the cross of Jesus). God's very essence is reaching and interactive love. God exists as Father, Son, and Spirit, a community of love and mutuality always reaching and relating. The biblical God is no lonely God, but a singular communion. God is a dynamic and loving triune being who wants to have meaningful interaction with us. God stands above (Father), stoops below (Son), and forever stays nearby (Spirit).

The trinitarian God is the one eternal God who was as trinitarian in the Old Testament as in the Incarnation or at Pentecost of the New. The God who is the pentecostal presence and gifting is the God of the burning bush encountered by Moses, the hot coals that touched the lips of Isaiah, and the little infant in the Bethlehem manger. The concept of "Trinity" arose from the spiritual experience of early disciples of Jesus who knew of only one God but were conscious of the very present lordship of the Risen Christ and the power of Christ's ever-present Spirit. –Clark H. Pinnock, *Most Moved Mover,* and Arthur Wainwright, *Trinity in the New Testament*

15. WHICH GENDER IS GOD?

Language shapes significantly how we think about things. Words reflect and construct reality for humans. What about speaking of God in particular gender language? The Bible clearly evolved in a patriarchal world, so masculine language tends to dominate. The Bible clearly reveals God as living, speaking, and personal, but never "he" nor "she" in essential being. The second commandment forbids humans making God in the image of any earthly thing, women or men included. The actual reality of God is beyond everything we humans can conceive (Isa. 55:8–9; 1Cor. 2:9–13). God reflects the best characteristics of each gender without being either.

When we speak about God as "Father," and the "Son" who comes to us in the man Jesus, and about the "Spirit" who is the Spirit of the Father and the Son, we are not talking about the gender of God. We are using language analogies from human experience to talk about the kind of relationships that exist between the members of the divine Trinity, and between the Triune God and us human beings. How careful we must be not to use our language analogies to be unjust to each other by insisting that one gender is superior to another. –Shirley C. Guthrie, *Christian Doctrine*

16. THERE'S NO BETTER PLACE!

Why did Jesus begin his model prayer for his disciples by addressing "Our Father"? It's because all things begin with and depend on the sovereign One, the liberating and saving One, the Messiah-sending One. The word *Father* is not meant to highlight any male dominance. It's intended to catch up all of the election, frustration, and expectation known about God and hoped for because of God across all of Jewish and Christian history. Jesus was saying to his disciples, "Let it be *now* and let it be *us!*" Begin your prayers, he taught, with "Our Father," the Father of Jesus and of Israel and of us too! This Father is Lord of lords, King of kings, the author of time, the bringer of salvation, and the master of eternity.

The Father is the only place to begin and the best possible place to end, to live and to die. What's the primary response of God to human suffering? It's God's personal identification with it *in Christ*. The main answer to the problem of pain is *the pain of God*. It's not that God is not *able* to do certain things. God's problem is that *God loves*! Love, we respectfully say, complicates the life of God as it does every life that truly loves. We typically speak of the sacrifice of Jesus when actually we should dare to say more. God in Jesus was *Self*-sacrificing as an amazing act of divine love. That's who God is. Therefore, that's the best and only place to begin our believing and to root our living and hoping. –Barry L. Callen, *The Jagged Journey* and *The Prayer of Holiness-Hungry People*

17. GOD'S BEST FLOWER IMAGE

I suggest a flower that speaks most biblically and is most pastorally satisfying in its description of God's nature and working with us humans. It's the ROSE. God is **R**elational, **O**pen, **S**uffering, and **E**verywhere active. God willingly, out of love, chooses to relate to the creation, being open to each human decision freely made, and suffering when the wrong ones are made. God always remains redemptive and engaged with all people on behalf of their reconciliation and fulfillment. Thanks be to God! Some leave the flower analogy and speak of ACURA. That is, (1) **A**ll are sinful, (2) **C**onditional election, (3) **U**nlimited atonement, (4) **R**esistible grace, and (5) **A**ssurance of salvation. This is the reverse of John Calvin's TULIP flower (total depravity, unconditional election, limited atonement, irresistible grace, and perseverance of the saints).

In Colossians 1:15 Paul insists that Jesus Christ is none other than God now becoming human for our salvation. Christ is the creative purpose that initially shaped all creation, remains supreme over all its orders of being, and is the unifying principle that underlies the whole cosmos and continues to hold it together. In short, Christ is the visible expression of the invisible God. To know the heart of God, *just look at Jesus*. What a verse! He is the ultimate presence of God in our midst, the full flowering of the divine ROSE. –Barry L. Callen, *The Heart of the Matter*

18. ONE GOD, MULTIPLE COLORS AND WILLS

What color is the holy God? Should God be painted black, tainted with the darkness that humans know so well? If not black, does that mean that the all-bright God is keeping the darkness real for some reason, delaying the shining of the great eternal light? God is best colored as *holy love*. God is at once the green of creation, the white of purity, and the red of redemption. God is the rainbow of sovereign, loving grace. His primary color is a brilliance dominated by all the hues of love. The delay in dispersing the darkness is motivated by a redemptive patience that's hard for us to fully understand.

Divine love is unchanging, but its strategies do change as circumstances shift because of human actions (Ps. 40:8, Matt. 6:10, Jn. 7:17). Such is the complexity and beauty of divine love. There are no limits on the freedom of divine action, except what arises from the very nature of God, which is love. The one God of love thus has *three wills*. 1. *Intentional*: none should be lost from God's loving care and all will be in the right relationship with God and each other now and eternally. 2. *Circumstantial*: God reluctantly allows and adapts to our many choices, good or bad, constantly working toward the intentional will. 3. *Ultimate*: persuasive love, as opposed to outright coercion, is how God typically works to achieve divine intentions in the face of bad human choices (Rom. 8:28). Nothing that happens can finally defeat the will of God. –Leslie Weatherhead, *The Will of God*

19. THE PARADOXICAL GOD WE SERVE

When seeking critical theological perspective, we should begin with the nature and ways of God as revealed in Scripture, and especially in the person of Jesus Christ. The Bible reveals God as voluntarily open to suffering on our behalf and demonstrates the divine Self as loving grace. There is an amazing *mutuality* about how God operates. God grants freedom of decision and reaches lovingly to all persons, enabling them to respond in ways that can bring eternal salvation. God risks negative outcomes by allowing choices against his will. Love requires freedom. What a wonderful God we are invited to serve!

A key teaching of John Wesley is that the God's power or sovereignty is to be understood fundamentally in terms of *empowerment* rather than control or over-powerment. This does not weaken God's power but determines its character. As Wesley was fond of saying, God works "strongly and sweetly." God's grace works powerfully but not irresistibly in human life and salvation. It empowers our *response-ability* without overriding our *responsibility*. God's grace is paradoxical, both *gift* and *task*. As a gift, God imputes righteousness to believers through the work of Jesus Christ. As a task, God intends those believers to respond in faith, hope, and love. Failing to respond is failing to really receive. –Randy L. Maddox, *Responsible Grace*

20. IT'S PARTY TIME!

Jesus' story of the "prodigal son" is surely about more than the wayward son who wasted his inheritance and finally begged forgiveness. It's about the father who, despite everything, welcomed the wayward home. In biblical times children were required to show utmost respect for parents. For the younger son to ask for his inheritance while the father was alive was basically saying to his father, "I wish you were dead!" Jewish hearers of this story would have been shocked and wonder mostly what the father would do to this awful child. What a picture of God! It's a picture of the loving and forgiving God in action. God is the Holy Sovereign who nonetheless functions as *active love*.

Nothing is deserved, but all is received. Prepare the best meal and praise the Father God. It's party time! The beloved hymn "Joy to the World" announces that Jesus "rules the world with truth and grace." The resurrected Jesus rules as God's appointed King over all things. He rules *with truth* and so is the dependable prophet and teacher of God. He rules with truth *and grace* as the divinely appointed priest who mediates between loving Creator and fallen creation. It's no wonder that this hymn concludes by calling us to "repeat the sounding joy!" –Barry L. Callen, *Beneath the Surface*

21. I REALLY *LIKE* THE GOD I *LOVE*

I *love* God for who God is and for what he has done for us, but also I *like* God for the ways God does things. When God makes the crown of his creation out of dirt, continually uses the least likely for his most important jobs, draws us near through bread and wine, and sneaks into the world as an infant, it's the sort of good-natured fun that makes me want to spend time with this God. I can't help but like a God who brings a mighty nation into being through an elderly and barren couple and then preserves that people with assistance from Esther, a beauty pageant winner.

When God extends forgiveness to those who don't deserve it, stands up for the powerless, and brings victory from sacrifice, I detect a winsomeness that enhances my enjoyment of the time I spend with God. I don't always understand God, but when I look at the way God does things through the filter of humor, I can't help but think of God as likable. I *love* this God and *like* him so much that I want to be with him and be like him. Look at David Elton Trueblood's book. The ultimate of God's presence with us humans, the sacrificed Son, was also the most curious way to get done the biggest thing of all. –Steve Wilkins, *What's So Funny about God?*, and David Elton Trueblood, *The Humor of Christ*

> This is my Father's world,
> Or let me ne'er forget,
> That though the wrong seems oft so strong,
> God is the ruler yet . . . (Maltbie D. Babcock)
>
> The Earth is the Lord's and the fullness thereof,
> the world and those who dwell therein;
> For He has founded in upon the seas
> and established it upon the rivers . . . (Psalm 24)

Great is Thy faithfulness, O God, my Father,
there is no shadow of turning with Thee;
Thou changest not, Thy compassions they fail not, as
Thou hast been Thou forever wilt be . . .
(Thomas Chisholm)

Oh, for a thousand tongues to sing,
my great Redeemer's praise . . . (Charles Wesley)

When I in awesome wonder, consider all the worlds
Thy hands have made . . . (Stuart K. Hine)

The King of love, my Shepherd is,
whose goodness faileth never . . . (Henry W. Baker)

There's a wideness in God's mercy
like the wideness of the sea . . . (Frederick W. Faber)

Be Thou, my vision,
O Lord of my heart . . . (Irish hymn)

Holy, holy, holy, Lord God Almighty,
Unto everlasting days our
song shall rise to Thee . . . (Reginald Heber)

I believe in God, the Father,
Mighty, yet the fount of love;
Maker of the whole creation,
earth below and heaven above . . . (Julie Tennent)

Merciful and mighty, God in three persons,
blessed Trinity . . . (Reginald Heber)

The Truths of God
For the People of God

He is the image of the invisible God, the first-born of all creation. . . . And the Word became flesh and lived among us and we have seen his glory, the glory as of a father's only son, full of grace and truth. (Col. 1:15-16; Jn. 1:14)

All things have been handed over to me by my Father, and no one knows the Son except the Father, and no one knows the Father except the Son and anyone to whom the Son chooses to reveal him. (Matt. 11:27)

II

The Son Who Fully Embodies

Who actually was and still is Jesus of Nazareth? He was badly misunderstood in his physical time on earth, and he still is. He was killed by those who misunderstood and were threatened by him. Even his closest disciples struggled to understand, even though Jesus spent considerable teaching time with them. His person and message were unexpected, shocking, and bigger that human minds can easily grasp. Books could not hold all the truth that he taught and that he was. A cross and a grave could not stop his life from going on forever!

Christian faith is centered in knowing the real Jesus and through that knowledge, and actual relationship with him through the Spirit, gaining intimacy with the presence and forgiveness of the God the Father. Being aware of what Jesus accomplished is key to our present and future spiritual lives. That awareness is as important as things can get! Following are twenty golden nuggets of Christian truth that illumine the problems and possibilities of coming to know and love the one real God through knowing and relating to his only Son, Jesus Christ.

Glimpses of the following Golden Nuggets

1. He came as the Composer of life bringing a brand new song.
2. You can't really know Jesus by analyzing "facts" about him.
3. It's something we can't explain but still must believe.
4. Exactly whose son is Jesus, God's or Mary's? Yes.
5. Jesus is *for us* but not *from us*, a very important distinction.

6. The resurrected Jesus is a symbol of the work of God.
7. Jesus had two distinct but never separate natures.
8. Jesus just is, always was, and in the end will yet be!
9. We are never left alone in our suffering.
10. A vision of God as active holiness changes everything!
11. We should be reaching in love to all without distinction.
12. We are Christians when Jesus is our source, center, and life.
13. We are to be clothed entirely in the Christ who is "all in all."
14. God in Christ is the divine mystery anxious to be understood.
15. We are to be active agents of Christ's resurrection.
16. "Atonement" has many faces, no one comprehensive.
17. Always try to satisfy people? Jesus didn't, we shouldn't try.
18. Here's language that will stop all mouths!
19. Why keep proclaiming Jesus to the whole world?
20. We are forgiven in Christ and enabled to live holy lives.

1. BRINGING A NEW SONG

Jesus wasn't the sort of king people in his day wanted. He was anything but what they had become used to expecting, a second-rate sort of king. They were looking for a builder to construct a home they thought they wanted, but he was the Architect coming with a new plan that would give them everything they needed. They were looking for a singer to sing the song they had been humming for a long time. He was the Composer bringing them a new song to which the old songs they knew were to be reduced to no more than background music.

Jesus was *the* King. He had come to redefine kingship itself around his own work, mission, and fate. It's now time to recognize not only who Jesus was in his own day, despite the failure of his contemporaries to recognize him, but also who he is and intends to be for our own day. "Jesus came to what was his own," wrote one of his great early followers, "and his own people did not accept him" (Jn. 1:11). That puzzle continues. We finite people are always caught off guard by the infinite. –N. T. Wright, *Simply Jesus*

2. JESUS IS SUBJECT, NOT OBJECT

We now are a data-driven society. We know by gathering all the records and numbers and then drawing our well-informed conclusions. That's not, however, how we can ever know God. God is Subject to be encountered, not object to be studied. We come to know God only as God gives himself to be known by us, and that's not by a complex spreadsheet. Jesus said God has given himself through the coming of the Son (Matt. 11:27; 1 Cor. 2:9-16). Knowing God hardly consists in a list of informational statements or theological propositions about heavenly matters. Since God is "Person," true knowledge of God requires an encountering of the searching person with the reaching Person in intimate contact. In that encounter and growing relationship with the Subject, God grasps us and helps us know ourselves as well as God.

The needful reality is not merely that I come to know God but that in the Person-to-person encounter God makes clear that I am known well and that God is prepared to enable me to deal with my lostness. Paul remarks to the Galatians, "but now that you know God—or rather are known by God" (Gal: 4:9). It isn't just that *God is* but that God is *with us* in Jesus Christ, wanting to be known and in that knowing wanting to save. Since Jesus is also divine Person, never to be reduced to any theological proposition about him, knowing God requires being in active relationship with Jesus, enabled by the biblical record and through his Spirit directly. –Stanley J. Grenz, *Theology for the Community of God*

3. AN AMAZING AND NECESSARY PARADOX

The term "incarnation" literally means "en-flesh-ment" and refers to a uniquely Christian belief. God has entered history in the form of a human person. "The word became flesh and dwelt among us" (Jn. 1:14). This is a foundation stone, a golden nugget on which the Christian faith stands or falls. The New Testament materials provide only the raw materials for a "Christology," that is, some full explaining of the relation between the human and divine within the one man, Jesus. The major councils and creeds of Christians over the centuries have resisted all proposed solutions that try to simplify the situation by compromising in any way either aspect of the dual nature of the person of Jesus. If he is not the God-man, fully and really, he is a fraud and nothing of significance for our faith.

Judging only by the best efforts of our human minds, we are left with this paradox. The human and divine aspects of the one person of Jesus are equally real and essential. They move together in a mysterious manner always a bit beyond our rational comprehension. The bottom line is this. The disciples of Jesus experienced Jesus as a fully human being, and at the same time they encountered in him the full presence of God. They experienced this amazing mystery and proclaimed it even though they were not able to fully explain it. They knew, as we must, that human salvation is based solidly on the person of Jesus, the God-man. "When you have seen me, you have seen the Father" (Jn. 14:9). –H. Ray Dunning, *Grace, Faith, & Holiness*

4. EXACTLY WHOSE SON IS HE?

Matthew and Luke alone in the New Testament report the virginal conception of Jesus. They don't say that Jesus was divine and sinless *by virtue* of this unusual conception, but they do signify belief in the full presence of God in the full story of Jesus. The point of the biblical story is that, from the very beginning of the earthly existence of Jesus, the Holy Spirit was the active agent in the dawning of a new age. It is God in Christ who makes possible our pardon, God who awakens in us our need of grace in Christ. The Bible makes this stunning declaration. Jesus *is* the eternal Word of God, not merely a teacher with a divine word to share. "The Word became flesh and lived among us" (Jn. 1:14). Jesus, the teacher of the Word, *is the Word!*

A wise lecturer posed this. "Your answer to this will tell me whether you have a gospel to preach or not. Was Jesus the son of Mary who became the Son of God? Or was he the eternal Son of God who became the son of Mary? If the first, you have no gospel. Salvation is in God alone. If Jesus emerged out of us, he can do nothing more for us than we could do for ourselves. But if he came to us out of the nature and by the initiative of the eternal Deity, then he can do for us what only God can do." The virginal conception is an *object* of faith, not its *foundation* as is the resurrection of Jesus. The mechanics of the baby's conception was at God's option. The resurrection had to be or everything Jesus taught and claimed died with him. –Dennis F. Kinlaw, *Lectures in Old Testament Theology,* and Stanley J. Grenz, *Theology for the Community of God*

5. FOR US BUT NOT FROM US!

We need to be sure of who Jesus was--and is--before we attempt to witness about him to others. Mark's Gospel gives us the basic story of Jesus. Matthew, Luke, and John then elaborate on this story in different ways for different readerships. Whatever their several differences, all agree on the most important thing. Jesus actually was *God with us*! Mark uses the word "immediately" forty-one times as he gallops from one event to another, anxious to tell this story quickly and with excitement. He reaches a high point when Jesus asks Peter who he thinks Jesus really was. The dramatic response, "You are the Christ, the Messiah!" (8:29).

That response is what Mark's story is all about, a real man becoming known as the One who came from God, in fact, in whom *God was with us*. Mark and the others soon would report that even the coming grave would not be able to hold Jesus! (16:6). Who exactly is Jesus? He's no less than God's Messiah, the One come from heaven to bring salvation to all who believe, the One who chose the way of the Suffering Servant foretold in Isaiah 53. Mark's account presents Jesus as the heavenly One who also was a real human being, God come *in the flesh*, the infinite God somehow for a brief time also finite, with us, one of us, for us, but not *from us*. –Barry L. Callen, *All of God's Word for All of My Needs*

6. JESUS THEN, NOW, AND ALWAYS!

Jesus said that seeing him constituted seeing God, his Father and ours. Especially in light of the resurrection of Jesus, we experience the tenacity of God with and for us. No defeat diminishes the divine resolve or ability to seek human good. In Jesus we see God as fully with us and clearly with us for our salvation. We see a patiently working God who inspires and enables the new and the better, often despite our misunderstanding and resistance. While sometimes bewildering and even possibly a little self-serving, we now have Christian theologies called womanist, open, process, liberation, evangelical, Black, and more. They all claim a Jesus origin. Without him, they are nothing but self-serving ideologies. With him, they are sincere attempts to penetrate divine truth on behalf of human good.

Each of these theological mind-sets insists in varying ways that God is fundamentally love, willing to be vulnerable, affected by our wayward world, determined to inspire more love and justice. In the midst of our sin, there is a directional power at work in what seems to be a purely contingent and even whimsical cosmic process. That power is God in Jesus and now in his Spirit, present to guide, enable, and save. We believing disciples are charged with the ongoing task of how best to order our attitudes and lives for the good of all persons and the creation itself. God remains in our midst to lure forward this redemptive process. Jesus was then, is now, and always will be! –Delwin Brown, *What Does a Progressive Christian Believe?*

7. REQUIRED UNITY IN INEVITABLE DIVERSITY

Christians believe that God is revealed uniquely in Jesus Christ and that the Bible is the uniquely inspired witness to Jesus Christ, and therefore to God. Christian theologians have used various models and metaphors to express the significance of Jesus Christ. Is there a basic, universal belief about Jesus inherent in all these diverse models and metaphors? Is there a criterion by which newly developed thought patterns should be judged so that there are not many Christs, only varying attempts to describe the one Christ? There is. It's the one agreed on by the leaders of early and undivided church.

The universal baseline is an outworking in formal language of the apostolic witness itself. *Jesus Christ is God incarnate, one unified person, the eternal Son of God equal with the Father, of two distinct but never separate natures, human and divine.* This unifying understanding is admittedly a mouth-full, a magnificent mystery. It does not say everything about Christ that needs to be said in particular cultures and contexts. It merely rules out as inappropriate anything that seeks to reduce Jesus to something less or other than "truly human and truly divine," the God-man who alone can be Savior of the world. –Roger E. Olson, *The Mosaic of Christian Belief*

8. BEFORE BEING WITH US, HE ALWAYS WAS!

The Gospel of John presents Jesus as the true Vine, the Bread of life, and the Light of the world. Rather than "Messiah," a Jewish concept unknown to the larger world, John pictures the identity of Jesus in non-Hebrew philosophic terms (1:1–18). In his narrative, the story of Jesus doesn't begin as a baby in Bethlehem but as one who always was the *Logos*, the Word, the eternal expression of the creative God now made flesh for our human salvation. There is a pre-existence stressed. "Before Abraham was, *I am*" (8:58). The glory that Jesus has with the Father existed before the world was created (17:5). All these amazing affirmations, however, are not at the expense of his being true humanity. Jesus, voluntarily and sacrificially, assumed the role of a suffering servant in the flesh for our human benefit.

Ours is an age of spiritual hungering that readily sheds old traditionalisms and religious institutions in favor of something more personal and supposedly more authentic. Are "moderns" patient enough to linger and search? Are we so practical that we want only what works quickly and obviously, without any complex philosophy or theology attached, and certainly with no confining religious trappings or claimed Jewish fulfillments? John presents Jesus relatively free of any religious establishment. Jesus just is, always was, and in the end will yet be, the eternal God with us! –Barry L. Callen, *All of God's Word for All of My Needs*

9. WE ARE NOT ALONE!

Christians have rightly emphasized the importance of viewing Jesus as both fully divine and fully human. In times of pain and suffering, rather than doubting the presence and love of God, people should look to Jesus. As Scripture says, God in the Son was empathizing with us, caring so much about the problems of evil, sin, pain, and suffering that he became present with us in the midst of the suffering. God came to earth in the person of Jesus to suffer with loved people and thus provide a way of escape from the effects of sin, condemnation and death.

The promise of eternal life may not seem sufficient to balance all the evil, sin, pain, and suffering that occurs. There is no way to minimize the injustices, violence, catastrophes, weeping, and sorrow people experience. What can be affirmed and celebrated is that God did not leave us to experience all this alone. God was fully with us in the past through the life, death, and resurrection of Jesus, and God continues to be with us in the present through the person and work of the Holy Spirit. We do not suffer alone. God is with us, comforting, encouraging, guiding, and empowering us to persevere. –Don Thorsen, *What's True about Christianity?*

10. A FRESH VISION OF GOD'S HOLINESS

If God is the high and holy loving Father, exactly like the Son in nature and purpose, then we can truly *love* God. Divine holiness, ultimate reality, pure love, is now God-revealed. God is what God does—and *Jesus is what God is and now has done*. Rather than being known primarily as perfect, unchangeable, wholly other, and timeless, the biblical emphases are on God as present, active, seeking relationships, and being voluntarily vulnerable to our self-destructive human decisions. Dare we say it as our ultimate act of faith? The name and nature of God *is Jesus!*

That vulnerable infant in the Bethlehem manger, and then the mature and forgiving man on that old rugged cross outside Jerusalem, reveals the very heart of God the Father. For a picture of God in action on our behalf, remember the sacrifice of Jesus on the cross and therefore understand that God's very nature is *loving grace*. This vision of divine holiness changes everything! –Barry L. Callen, *Christian Holiness,* and *God As Loving Grace*

11. JESUS FOR ALL THE PEOPLE

Luke's writing in his Gospel and its extension in the Book of Acts is a beautiful portrayal of a boundary-breaking faith moving across frontiers and over time in the power of God's Spirit. In this Gospel there appear the classic stories of the Prodigal Son and Good Samaritan. Jesus is shown reaching to the black sheep of the society of that day, including women, lepers, and the poor. We see him focusing on prayer and meditation to sustain himself in his frantic schedule and against significant opposition. Despite all the negatives, there's joy everywhere in Luke's account, especially in the *Magnificat* (1:46–55), the *Benedictus* (1:68–79), and Simeon's song, *Nunc Dimittis* (2:29–32).

There's limited theological interest featured in Luke's writings. He's more pragmatic, a sensitive doctor focusing on the details of human hurting and healing, always pointing to Jesus, the great Friend, Healer, and Savior of all humanity. He reports Jesus in Nazareth announcing his mission "to bring good news to the poor, to proclaim release to the captives and recovery of sight to the blind, to set free those who are oppressed" (4:18). The Christian faith always should be reaching in love to all people without distinction, and doing so with the dignity of a Luke who tells the sweet story of the love of God come in Jesus for all people. –Barry L. Callen, *All of God's Word for All of My Needs*

12. WHO REALY IS A CHRISTIAN?

A Christian is one who becomes convinced that the fact of Jesus Christ is the most important and trustworthy thing to be known by us humans. And what about him is the fact? We come to trust him to reveal accurately the very being and character of God, the possibility of miracle, the meaningfulness of prayer, and the life everlasting. We are convinced that Jesus was not wrong about his report of himself. He said, "All things have been delivered to me by the Father, and no one knows the Father except the Son" (Matt. 11:27). We come to believe that knowing Christ brings wisdom in all other areas of life.

Jesus is not merely the greatest figure in human history or the finest of moral teachers. The Christian affirms the understanding that he is the genuine revelation of the mystery of our very existence, the one clear light among the many shadows. Further, commitment to him means much more that our admiration of him and the championing of his ideas. It's to share with him when he says, "I am the resurrection and the life" (Jn. 11:25). It means our passionate involvement in his life, teachings, death, and resurrection. We are hardly Christians until we truly are committed to these amazing facts and living into these transformative possibilities. –D. Elton Trueblood, *A Place to Stand*

13. A SUPREME BIBLE PASSAGE

Colossians 3:12–17 is certainly a highlight New Testament passage. Jesus of Nazareth is the "cosmic Christ." In his resurrection and return to his Father's right hand, he has become head of the church, his body, while continuing to be Master of the whole universe. He is the full image of God who is calling followers to a new way of life rooted in and inspired by Jesus. The "peace of Christ" is to rule in our hearts, and the "word of Christ" is to dwell in us richly. All false teachings are to be swept aside. All fear of unseen powers is to be abandoned.

Their replacements are to be a vivid portrait of what it looks like to be formed in the image of Christ and to live as one clothed entirely in the Christ who is "all in all." Note Colossians 1:15-20, another supreme passage presenting the amazing identity of Jesus the Christ. No wonder John Wesley could pray: "O Thou Who camest from above, the pure celestial fire to impart, kindle a flame of sacred love on the altar of my heart!" –Barry L. Callen, with Steve Hoskins, *A Year with Rabbi Jesus,* vol. 1

14. ANOTHER SUPREME BIBLE PASSAGE

Ephesians 3:1-12 is another supreme "Christological" passage. Paul admits that knowing God is a search for mystery, but a marvelous mystery that (Who) wants to be found, indeed, was made known to Paul and now to us by personal divine revelation. "Mystery" television shows and novels keep us guessing until the end about who did some awful thing. In the case of God in Jesus, the mystery keeps dropping clues so that we may be found by the great mystery. Our moment of "epiphany" comes when we realize we are the hunted, the one sought in love by God to bring us to fullness of life. The awful thing done, the cross of Jesus, was done *for us,* not against us or even by us! The mystery is fully enfolded in the infant Jesus who now is to be proclaimed with boldness and confidence as the heart of creation itself.

Here's the divine mystery in a nutshell, the plot of the ages being revealed. The community of Jesus, guided by his Spirit (Eph. 3:5) and enabled by God's grace (Eph. 3:2, 7–8) has received the mystery of God's being and will (Eph.1:9) for the purpose of making it known (Eph. 3:8). That community of faith, the church, becomes God's people by receiving with gladness the mystery of God with us in Jesus. It remains the church as it embodies and communicates to the whole world the gladness of this marvelous mystery now revealed. –Barry L. Callen, with Steve Hoskins and Jonathan Powers, *A Year with Rabbi Jesus,* vol. 2

15. WE ARE THE "FORCE FIELD" OF RESURRECTION!

The three Abrahamic religions, Judaism, Christianity, and Islam see God as the one "who brings the dead to life and calls into being what does not exist" (Rom. 4:17). For Christians, this pattern of incarnation, death, and resurrection is supremely revealed in "the Christ mystery" that was active long before Jesus of Nazareth. It functioned from the very birth and death of the stars to the entire circle of all life on this planet. It then became enfleshed in Jesus and the Easter center of our faith. In Christ, all of creation is divinely conceived, beloved of God, crucified, and potentially reborn. Resurrection is a big neon sign that keeps alluring and inviting history forward toward its certain conclusion.

The risen Christ is the divine lure, a brilliant light set as the omega point of time and history. He keeps reminding us that love, not death, is the great eternal reality. Once we are truly in Christ, there no longer is any fear of death. We have been there and back, crucified already (Rom. 6:6). The risen Christ in us always knows that it will never lose anything real by dying. Our task and privilege as spiritually resurrected people is to take our place in the "force field" of resurrection (Phil. 2:11–12). We know that the life-giving God is at work in us. The breathing into Adam (Gen. 2:7) has become the breathing out of Jesus (Jn. 20:22). His breathing on us is for us to receive the Holy Spirit and become the Spirit's agents of new life.
–Richard Rohr, *Immortal Diamond*

16. JESUS OUR ATONEMENT

In response to the sin and broken relationship which have alienated God from people, many stories, images, and analogies are found in Scripture. They are attempts to describe how God has provided humanity with the opportunity for salvation—for forgiveness, healing, reconciliation, and growth, as well as for eternal life. These various biblical presentations are pictures of how people may humanly understand, at least in part, what God has done to restore their relationships with one another and with God.

No single picture (story, image, or analogy) is sufficient to describe the fullness of what Jesus accomplished on behalf of people in order to enable this restoration, but together they help to communicate the full gospel to which God wants people to respond. One of the most common words used to describe God's provision for people's restoration is *atonement*. The early English language meaning of the word implied "at-one-ment," that is, reconciliation between people or between people and God. – Don Thorsen, *What's True about Christianity?*

17. ADAM TWO REVERSES ADAM ONE

Even though Jesus was meeting the needs of people in amazing ways, he did not come as a servant *of people*. He came as a servant *of God* and in that service ministering to people. God's agenda directed his activities. Two major dynamics are at work in the Christian servant-Master relationship. The nature of the servants is transformed to reflect the Master, and the priorities of the servants are realigned to please the Master. The nature of Jesus reflected God the Father perfectly so that when we "see him we have seen the Father." His priorities were completely guided by his Father's business. Jesus surrendered his own human agenda in order to fulfill the agenda of his Father at whatever the earthly cost.

In this complete sacrifice of Jesus, the Second Adam reversed the effects of the first Adam. The first chose selfishly to assert his own will, "not your will but *mine* be done." The second chose selflessly to submit to God's will, "not my will, but *yours* be done." Herein is the path we are called to follow as servant disciples of the Master. We minister freely to people, but only in the process of loyalty to the mission of our Father. People often have expectations and demands we will not meet. That's the sacrifice of serving only one Master and not frantically trying to always satisfy two. –Kevin W. Mannoia, *Expressing Life*

18. LANGUAGE TO STOP ALL MOUTHS!

John's Gospel is organized around a series of key "signs," each culminating in an "I Am!" (*ego eimi*) statement. They reflect similar self-identifying statements of Yahweh in the Old Testament. They speak of oneself as actually God! When Jesus raised a dead man, he said, "I *am* the resurrection and the life" (Jn. 11:25). In giving sight to the man born blind, Jesus said, "I *am* the light of the world" (Jn. 8:12). When he fed the five thousand, he declared, "I *am* the bread of life" (Jn. 6:35). He later said, "I *am* the door of the sheep" (Jn. 10:7) and "I *am* the good shepherd" (10:10).

These are extremely immodest statements, if applied to an ordinary human subject, would be outrageous. And yet, Jesus did not teach as the prophets before him taught when they pointed beyond themselves to the divine source of their revelations. Rather, he taught and spoke in the first person, as Yahweh had spoken in the form of "I Am" in the Exodus account of deliverance. Martin Luther thought that by this means Jesus deliberately used language "to stop all mouths." If his self-identifications were false, he was deluded and deserving of the death he received. If they were true, his very person and presence were history shattering and God unveiling!
–Thomas C. Oden, *Classic Christianity*

19. WE CAN'T HELP BUT PROCLAIM!

Why a figure from so long ago still being actively proclaimed worldwide as the most important person ever born? There are four reasons and they never go away. First, there is the command of Jesus himself. "All power is given to me in heaven and in earth. Go, therefore, and teach all nations" (Matt. 28:18–19). If one believes this stunning statement, going everywhere then seems inevitable. Second is the urgency of the situation. The end of the world might not be far ahead and a lost world is perishing for lack of the good news. Time has shown that all human systems of religious belief, societal governance, and human fulfillment are deeply flawed. They all need Jesus–now!

There's more. The original disciples had encountered something—Someone—well beyond anyone who ever before had burst onto the human scene with such force. There was the wonder of his forgiveness, the power of his spoken word, the sheer glory of his message about God. God is not unknowable, jealous, fickle, threatening, but now known *in Jesus* as pure love reaching to save, a reality beyond the world's fondest dreams! Says a Greek proverb, "They who have the torch must pass on the light." Jesus is the Light of the world! And then the fourth reason for proclamation. There was and is the profound belief of all true disciples that *"JESUS IS LORD!"* (Acts 2:26, Rom. 10:9, 1 Cor. 12:3). Beyond teaching the great truths, Jesus *is the truth*. He actually is God actually with us for our salvation now and forever! –James S. Stewart, *The Life and Teaching of Jesus Christ*

20. GOD'S ACTION AND OUR RESPONSE

A paradox is rooted in the nature of God. It is the nature of God to be irreconcilably opposed to sin; it is the nature of God to love sinners and seek reconciliation with them. No one but God could resolve the problem, and God himself could be faithful to both aspects of his being only at the cost of the Cross. While Christ's death is *sufficient* to atone for the sins of all, it is only *efficient* for those who have faith in Christ and in his sacrifice. There is an important enablement and expectation associated with this "efficiency" of our response to the work of Jesus on our behalf.

The effects of the death of Jesus amount not just to gaining us right standing with God, but also freeing us from the bondage of sin, cleansing us from sin, cleansing our consciences from guilt, and enabling us to live sanctified and holy lives that glorify God and edify our fellow human beings. "Atonement" is another way of talking about salvation. As Titus 2:11 says, "The grace of God *has appeared*, bringing *salvation to all*, training us to renounce impiety and worldly passions and in the present age to live lives that are self-controlled, upright, and godly while we await the blessed hope." –C. K. Barrett, *Romans*, and Ben Witherington, III, in *Wesleyan Theological Journal* (2015)

What child is this who, laid to rest,
on Mary's lap is sleeping? . . . (William C. Dix)

Come, O thou Traveler unknown,
Whom still I hold but cannot see.
With Thee all night I mean to stay,
And wrestle till the break of day . . . (Charles Wesley)

Christ is made the sure foundation,
Christ, the head and cornerstone . . . (Latin hymn)

God, the Father's only Son, yet with him
in glory one; one in wisdom, one in might,
absolute and infinite . . . (Samuel Stone)

I stand amazed in the presence of Jesus,
the Nazarene, and wonder how he could love me,
a sinner, condemned, unclean . . . (Charles Gabriel)

Born Thy people to deliver,
Born a child and yet a King,
Born to reign in us forever,
Now Thy gracious kingdom bring . . . (Charles Wesley)

And now for me He stands
before the Father's throne,
and shows His wounded hands,
and names me as his own . . . (Norman J. Clayton)

Light revealed through clouds of pain,
that the blind might see again;
Love content in death to lie,
that the dead might never die . . . (Samuel Stone)

I will sing the wondrous story of the Christ
who died for me, how he left his home in glory
for the cross of Calvary . . . (Francis H. Rowley)

Veiled in flesh the Godhead see,
Hail the incarnate Deity . . . (Charles Wesley)

Jesus, thou art all compassion,
pure, unbounded love thou art.
Visit us with thy salvation,
enter every trembling heart . . . (Charles Wesley)

All hail the power of Jesus name!
Let angels prostrate fall;
Bring forth the royal diadem,
and crown him Lord of all . . . (Edward Perronet)

The Truths of God
For the People of God

Then, Jesus interpreted to them the things about himself in all the Scriptures. . . . Jesus answered, "It is written, 'man shall not live by bread alone, but by every word that comes from the mouth of God'." (Lk. 24:27; Matt. 4:4)

Do not think that I have come to abolish the Law or the Prophets; I have come not to abolish, but to fulfill. . . . For the word of God is living and active, sharper than any two-edged sword. (Matt. 5:17; Heb. 4:12)

III

The Book that Properly Records

The Bible is the autobiography of the pioneer people of God in their pilgrimage of faith. It's the primary source for our knowing the story of the real God who now has come to us in Jesus, God's Son. It's the divinely "inspired" (inbreathed) history of God's calling of and being with the chosen people. It's the place to go today for believers to listen for the current speaking and continued inbreathing of the Spirit of God on all who read humbly with open spiritual ears and hearts.

Our task of biblical interpretation is to hear the Spirit's voice and not merely echoes of ourselves. The evil one is skilled at quoting Scripture for his own purposes, and too often we hear him clearly. Following are seventeen golden nuggets that provide key truths about the sacred Scriptures that help guide responsible interpretation. They now are entrusted to us by the ever-speaking God. Do we study with care and celebrate with joy this amazing gift of divine revelation? Do we indulge our private curiosities or welcome God's priorities? We must hear humbly *from above*!

Glimpses of the following Golden Nuggets

1. Those of us who have access to a Bible are privileged!
2. Is the silence of the Bible today really that deafening? Why?
3. The Bible might not be all we want, but it's sufficient.
4. What we have is an extensive religious library that's human and divine.

5. The "Protestant Principle" is a wise guide for more than Protestants.
6. The biblical pages present the God who really is and who we can be.
7. If you think the Bible is dull, look again!
8. The Bible was and still is sufficient because of the work of the Spirit.
9. Let's think of the first Testament as "Foundational" and not as "Old."
10. Did God get "saved" only when Jesus was born?
11. Why would Christians waste their time engaging in a battle for the Bible?
12. The earth is not flat and the Bible also has a varied texture.
13. The Bible sometimes *reports* things it does not *teach*. Be careful here.
14. The Bible is exceptional indeed, but not everything.
15. We are so practiced at misusing the Bible, making it say conflicting things.
16. To read and be reshaped by the Bible, we need the voice of the Spirit.
17. John Wesley is a dependable guide as we approach the sacred pages.

1. WE HAVE A DEPENDABLE REPORT OF JESUS!

If God has revealed fully the divine nature and intentions only in the person of Jesus Christ, we then struggle with this fact. A large percentage of humanity has never received a direct and convincing witness to Jesus. Even so, the Bible suggests that a loving God will seek to bring some awareness of himself to all people regardless of their restricted circumstances. God will not judge negatively those who never heard and never knew. Christian theologians speak of "general" as well as specific revelation. For instance, God's amazing creation is itself a witness to the loving divine, although admittedly a partial and sometimes misleading revelation.

The Gentiles (non-Jews) may not have had the Law enjoyed by the Jews, but somehow they had it written on their hearts and thus could manage to do what the Law requires (Rom. 2:14-16). The harmony, order, and beauty found in nature is a reflection of their creative source, God, known by whatever name. We Christians are convinced with Paul that God finally and fully has addressed us humans, and been with us personally "in the face of Jesus Christ" (2 Cor. 4. 4:5). The whole story surrounding this glorious face is available to us dependably in the Bible's report. Thank God for the specific revelation in the Bible! –Thomas N. Finger, *Christian Theology*

2. WE HAVE BECOME DIS-ENCHANTED

In the first quarter of the 21st century, the silence of the Bible has seemed deafening. Even in the so-called "Christian" countries of North America and Europe, the Bible now is rarely quoted in public. Speech is no longer seasoned with references to biblical texts. Parents don't quote Scripture to their children. Even in the churches, there is a strange and eerie biblical silence. Few people are involved in direct study of the Bible. Evangelical churches have little tolerance for the public reading of Scripture passages that contain more than a few verses. Preaching often has been reduced to sound bites from the Bible and then essays on current affairs and successful living.

This cultural disenchantment with the Bible correlates with the "Enlightenment" project of disenchanting the whole world. Focus is on the "natural laws" that can be discovered, understood, and harnessed for the betterment of life. Divine revelation, after all, could be only a figment of a church's lofty imagination. This self-centered secular vision has gradually stripped the world of belief in its being under the control of a supernatural power. As a result, people have lost a sense of the sacredness of the natural order. Creation has become an object to be acted on, lorded over, and conquered. It's time to rediscover the Bible as sacred, dangerous, and mysterious! It needs "re-enchanted." –Cheryl Bridges Johns, *Re-Enchanting the Text*

3. THE ADEQUATE AND ONGOING WITNESS

The Bible is the sufficient and adequate witness to God's self-disclosure to Israel and in Jesus Christ. Other sources of the study of God—tradition, reasoning, and experience—are of real value. However, they remain essentially dependent on Scripture since they must appeal to it for the very data they are remembering and on which they are reflecting. Granted, in biblical materials like the psalms it's hard to discover much systematic theological thinking. People are expressing their faith or lack of faith in God arising from a whole range of experiences in their lives. Even so, there is embedded in these materials a rather coherent set of ideas about God, humanity, and the world.

Scripture remains the central source of the memories, symbol systems, hopes, teachings, metaphors, and paradigms by which the Christian community originally came into being and has continually refreshed and renewed itself. The interpretive witness the Spirit of God did not completely cease with the canonization of Scripture but continues providing a guiding light for our understanding, experiencing, and applying. New events emerge in the ongoing historical process that are to be understood in light of the eternal Word made known in Scripture. The Spirit continues to enlighten, interpret, and teach. No fundamentally new or different knowledge is required beyond that which already is revealed in Scripture. –Thomas C. Oden, *Classic Christianity,* and Dennis F. Kinlaw, *Lectures in Old Testament Theology*

4. THE DIVINE-HUMAN LIBRARY

Sometimes approaching the Bible involves a hard choice between understanding it as a *human* book, in which the divine element is virtually eliminated, or as a *divine* book in which human elements are denied or explained away. In fact, the Bible is a divine-human library of "books," quite human and yet somehow also truly God's revelation, foundational and unchanging. Don't run from this paradox. Sometimes paradox is where the biggest truths hide.

The Bible was composed by frail humans and yet is a living document with divine relevance for the present. It needs to be freshly interpreted and applied in new circumstances by wisdom of the same Spirit who originally was its inspiration. Never forget, however, that Jesus is the full Word in flesh and his Spirit is the final interpreter of the many words in the Bible. We are to focus on reading and hearing God's Spirit guiding to personal maturity in Christ. We must not play games with the sacred text, allowing our personal preferences and curiosities and today's passing headlines to determine the truth that's found for us. –Barry L. Callen, *Caught Between Truths*

5. THE PROTESTANT PRINCIPLE

Negatively put, the "Protestant Principle" forbids anything human a place of ultimacy in the church. No creed, organizational structure, person or group of persons, no custom, habit, or idea, nothing human is to be allowed supremacy. Positively put, the Protestant Principle puts forward the absolute sovereignty of God expressed in the gospel of Jesus Christ. Our commitment is to be to the sovereignty of divine grace, not to any particular expression of it or theological reflection on it. Since many things are constantly trying to assume control in church life, Protestantism insists that reformation must be an ongoing characteristic of church life.

This Protestant Principle includes not making an idol of the Bible itself. Scripture is no ultimate merely as a written document. Although it's the primary vehicle of Christian truth, it's not the ultimate truth itself. It's the reliable source of information and instruction concerning the one true God and what it means to believe in him. But even here, the reliability of Scripture is understood to lie not in its mere words. The Protestant Principle insists that Scripture becomes binding for faith and practice only through the internal witness of the Holy Spirit. Scripture speaks savingly only as the Spirit enlivens it and witnesses to its truth. Apart from this witness of the Spirit, the Bible is only another religious book. –Paul M. Bassett, in *Wesleyan Theological Society*

6. THE BIBLICAL STORY OF GOD'S LOVE

Our conception of God has a tremendous impact on our lives individually and corporately. If we view God as essentially loving, then our ultimate concerns will be different than if we view God as essentially sovereign, judgmental, and aloof. A view of God as actively at work in the world will produce a much different way of viewing things than if we view God as essentially uninvolved. How we conceive God impacts more than our theology. It also influences how we see ourselves in responsible relationship with the world in which we live. Each person comes from a different background and set of life experiences, and thus has a particular story of God that might be spiritually positive, negative, or neutral.

Although Scripture is full of descriptions of God as all-powerful, all-knowing, and all-present, its preeminent way of describing God is that of *all-love*. The trajectory of Scripture intends to present God as one who wants to have loving fellowship with people—to forgive, restore, and heal from all that oppresses. God is still sovereign; God is still holy; God is still all the other attributes that Scripture uses for God. They are to be understood, however, in the context of an all-prevailing love. –Don Thorsen, *An Exploration of Christian Theology* and *What's True about Christianity?*

7. WHO SAID THE BIBLE IS DULL?

Dull? Open your Bible again and see if you can find these stories. A sperm-free pregnancy, a talking donkey with great vision, God arranging his prophet's marriage to a prostitute, ancient flying saucers that maybe were God, a little diarrhea to bring on romance, the queen parading nude in public except for her crown. Then there's a tent peg driven through a sleeping guy's head by a hostess who had just served him a nice dinner, bags of dirt guaranteeing an intimate meeting with God, the dumbest of all land deals, skeletons even in God's closet, and more.

Do you want to know how to be in this world *as God is*, have the mind in you *that Christ has*? Then read the Bible and see if you can find these stories. Read them with your eyes, listen carefully with your heart, preferably on your knees, and you'll find that God is still speaking! The Spirit opens up to the faithful reader a controlled liberty of interpretation of what is timely and crucial (liberty) as well as what is unchangingly true (orthodox). The text is not dead but alive with the Spirit for each of us in each new moment. –Barry L. Callen, *Bible Stories for Strong Stomachs*

8. THE SUFFICIENCY OF SCRIPTURE

Perhaps the best word to describe the nature and authority of the Bible in church history is "sufficiency." This word has the advantage of being found in Scripture. For example, in talking about how his prayers for healing did not result in healing, at least not as he had hoped, the apostle Paul reports that God said to him: "My grace *is sufficient* for you, for power is made perfect in weakness" (2 Cor. 12:9). We Christians should be content with the Bible that God has given us and not fancy it the way we wish it were or others say it is or at least should be. It might be nice to have an "inerrant" Bible, a "perfect" text errorless in all ways, but this concept appears to be mostly wishful thinking projected on the Bible by modernistic arguments not found in the sacred text itself.

The Holy Spirit who originally moved people to speak in ways that led to the biblical writing (2 Pet. 1:20-21) is the same Spirit who now guarantees the *sufficiency* of the Bible for God's intent and our spiritual needs today. That's why the "inductive" approach to Bible study is valuable. It encourages the present interpreter of the Bible to remain open to new learning and insights that may be different from previous ones that may have been shaped by the experiences and conclusions of others, results that don't fit with current facts. –Don Thorsen and Keith Reeves, *What Christians Believe about the Bible,* Don Thorsen, *What's True about Christianity?*, and Robert A. Traina and David R. Bauer, *Inductive Bible Study*

9. DROP "OLD" AND "NEW" TESTAMENTS

In order to be a true *biblical* Christian, we need to walk again that road to Emmaus with Jesus. He explained to confused Jews on the way an informed and fulfilled faith, the fuller Word from God, an updated understanding of their own religious tradition. "Beginning with Moses and all the prophets, Jesus interpreted for them the things about himself in all the Scriptures" (Lk. 24:27). Paul, a well-trained Jew, may have written large portions of the New Testament, but the inner world of his thought was primarily his Jewish heritage. Quotes and images from that previous heritage are numerous in the final biblical book, John's *Revelation.*

To really understand Scripture requires a Jesus explanation. The Jews on the road to Emmaus knew the "old" but required the "new" for real understanding. Therefore, I prefer that we avoid using words like "Old" and "New" for the two biblical testaments. That will remove improper negative connotations of the "Old." I suggest the "Foundational" and "Final" Testaments. Neither is really understood apart from the other. Both are inspired by God and yet relevant when interpreted through Jesus, the ultimate revelation. Only as a whole is the Bible properly considered the inspired and fully sufficient Word of God. If we claim it all as "inspired," let's not tag the bulk of it as "old." Granted, some of it now is clearly outdated, but it all retains value in fully understanding the many parts that never will be outdated. –Barry L. Callen, *Beneath the Surface*

10. AND GOD SAID, "MASSACRE EVERYTHING"?

My fundamentalist friends say that if an early writing in the Bible says that God told the Israelites to massacre all the Amalekites, including their children and cattle (Deut. 25), then God really did say and mean just that. In other words, God sometimes is in favor of genocide, at least of people God doesn't like. Granted, it's difficult to see how such a God is like the God Jesus has revealed, who is merciful and requires love even of enemies (Matt. 5). Did God take a course in Christian moral ethics between Deuteronomy and Matthew? Something certainly seems to have changed. One New Testament scholar says that God didn't get "saved" only when Jesus was born! God always has been the same. If so, apparently it's our understanding that's changed.

We must be careful when longing for the "old-time" religion. Some people dream about the golden age of the Catholic Church when heretics could be burned at the stake, literature could be censored, and salvation could be obtained by the payment of a small sum of money. Other people dream about the golden age of the Protestant Reformation when Catholics could be burned at the stake, people fined for not going to church, and all Catholics, Jews, and Muslims were sent to hell (so it was assumed, at least). How much our times and settings influence our Bible reading! –Keith Ward, *Confessions of a Recovering Fundamentalist*

11. WASTED ENERGY, LOST MISSION

Do you remember the various battles that have divided us Christians in recent generations? They include the worship battles, denominational battles, and certainly the battle for the Bible? What were we thinking? Sure, there has been a little good come out of all this struggling, but one surely could say that, while evangelicals were fiddling with petty arguments over things like "inerrancy" versus "infallibility" of the Bible, drums or hymnals in worship, the world was burning! Bickering over fine points inside the church can be a disaster for our mission outside the church.

We must stop using our energy defending our various "flavors" of viewpoint and shift rather to building healthy churches and their vigorous mission. Serious conversations over differences of viewpoint on the Bible's nature and teachings always are appropriate in church life–if they aren't allowed to obstruct mission and divide the Body of Christ in ways Jesus never meant. –Kevin Mannoia, *Church 2K*

12. THE BIBLE'S DEEP TEXTURE AND INTENT

The Earth is not flat, nor is the biblical text. It has depth, hills and valleys, movement and progress. It's closed in that we can't add new material. It's also open in that the Spirit of God hovers over the lines and words and continues to work and look forward, illuminating the relevance of the biblical text in circumstances and times far removed from its original composition. God's Word is unchanging in character and intentions, while also in a sense always a work in progress. Some of the Bible's deepest meanings only come to the surface of our understanding over time.

Jesus redirected various biblical texts to reflect the meanings of his coming, not to destroy but to reveal the deeper intent and enduring significance of the texts (Matt. 5:17). Matthew places fresh interpretation on Isaiah 7:14, one that Isaiah wouldn't have recognized but not thereby wrong. God continues to illumine what was first inspired, revealing its surplus of the Bible's meaning and relevance. One thing is constant throughout the Bible. It's intended to lead the reader to an understanding of and encountering with the God who speaks through these biblical materials in order to transform as humans back to God's original intent for us and the whole creation. Sometimes the full and present meaning of a text lies beneath the words and between the lines. Sometimes that deeper meaning isn't seen until shined upon by the great Light who is Jesus. –Barry L. Callen, *Beneath the Surface*

13. THE PERMANENT IN THE PASSING

When reading the Bible, there is need to distinguish between what it sometimes *reports* and what it intentionally *teaches*. There's a very important distinction here. The intentional teachings are what remain authoritative for Christians, and often these lie beneath the surface of the literal biblical text. Especially in the Foundational (Old) Testament, much is only reported. The deliberate teachings are necessarily expressed in the culture and language of the time. The texts contain values and theological truths that transcend their particular manners of expression. We must be on the lookout for the *permanent* teaching couched in the phrasing of the *passing*. Only the Spirit of God can guide dependably this delicate process.

There are intentional themes appearing throughout the Bible. God has chosen a people, unworthy partners for the most worthy of purposes (*covenant*). This people is to reflect God's own life among themselves and before all people (*holiness*). We are to order our lives as God has ordained (*with all the doubts and questions*).

Meanwhile, God will enable a radical hope that will sustain us in the most negative of circumstances (*a messiah*). God is the one and only source of the very water of life. This life-water flows through these intentional truth streams. The entire biblical text is to be understood in light of these pivotal "ways" of God. One of them lies beneath every biblical text. They are the permanent in the passing. –Barry L. Callen, *Beneath the Surface*

14. THE BIBLE ISN'T EVERYTHING

The Bible is much but not enough by itself. The reality is that God's Word is more than the singularity of the written Bible, more than the biblical words. Our human words are our expressions that flow from within. When we consider the Word of God as expressions of God, suddenly a new panorama opens. Genesis reports six times when God "expressed." The results were visible manifestations of God's creative imagination, each showing us some aspect of God's nature and heart. There are many ways to express ourselves. We get that from our Creator who has done the same thing.

God continued to express the God-self throughout the history of Israel, as witnessed in Scriptures by the prophets, priests, psalmists, and political leaders. God continues to express in the New Testament reports, principally through Jesus, the living Word. This line of thinking is not an effort to undermine the authority and primacy of Scripture as both a critical source of truth pointing us to God and a referent that validates other sources of truth. Taken together, however, God has expressed his nature and loving will in so many ways that are available to us. We should not miss any opportunity to discover God's revelation from whatever source it comes. –Kevin W. Mannoia, *Expressing Life* and an "*Anchored & Reaching*" podcast

15. FOCUS ON LIFE, NOT WORDS

The best "proof" of the truth of biblical revelation is in the combination of the actual *being* and *doing* of the Christian life. Confidence comes from concrete and consistent embodiment of stated beliefs. The biggest challenge facing today's theology and church is not *translation* but *enactment*. It's less what we say or exactly how we say it and more *what we do*. Our language about God dare not be mocked by our actual lives in the world. Words are fragile, actions are telling.

We must take seriously and exclusively our attachment to God the Father as known in Christ the Son (Matt. 7:14, 8:18-22, 10:34-39). We also must heed Paul's warning that we not be conformed to the values and power arrangements of this evil age (Rom. 12:2). We can be "biblical" in our own minds while believing however we want, acting in ways quite unlike Christ while still excusing it as biblical. We too often quote and use Scripture more than truly understand and submit to it. Too many Christians say they believe only what the Bible says, while actually believing what *they understand the Bible to say*. We can use the Bible to support slavery, the subjugation of women, capital punishment, capitalism, or the opposites of these. There's more at work here than our simple reading and believing the biblical text. –Barry L. Callen, *Beneath the Surface*

16. THE SPIRIT CONTINUES TO INTERPRET

Listen to the paraphrased instruction of Rabbi Jesus to his disciples. "Don't go out on my mission alone or try to read the inspired biblical pages alone, ignoring the interpretive wisdom of my Spirit and my people. Reading is done best in the community of faith. Individualism will be a future heresy in the church. To read my Word properly, and especially to see the signs of the times and the best current applications of its teachings, you'll need the eyes of the church and the voice of my Spirit. My Spirit is anxious to continue teaching you on my behalf. Read carefully and continue listening closely."

The Bible stands at the center of Christian faith, revealing the amazing reality of Rabbi Jesus. We must receive this divine mystery while realizing that the Bible's intent is more "formational" than "informational." Search its pages not to become experts in religious knowledge or future events but for yourself to be *re-shaped in the image of Christ*. The Bible is not an object over which we have control or a tool to be used at our whim. Instead, we should view the text as an instrument of God's grace in our lives intended to assist us in the critical process of our becoming conformed to the image of Christ. Always relate to it humbly with this in mind. –M. Robert Mulholland, Jr., *Shaped by the Word*

17. GUIDELINES FROM A WISE BIBLE READER

For John Wesley, the Scriptures are a reliable and sufficient guide to the Christian life. The truth of the Bible corresponds with what it intends to say about the history of salvation, not about incidental details or subjects of our mere curiosity. Wesley followed the Anglican article of faith that refers to the sufficiency and reliability of the Bible "in all things pertaining to salvation." He and we don't have to defend the truth of Scripture in areas that it never meant to address. The revealed Word is the basis of our Christian beliefs. We are not to discard parts of Scripture simply because we find them disagreeable.

Wesley said he would be convinced that he had misunderstood the biblical text if his reading did not prove itself in practical experience. He also made clear that one does not have the luxury of creating doctrine that is plainly contrary to the general sense of Scripture as a whole. One of his criticisms of mysticism was that it was "not being guided by the written word." The result of an experience-guidance that "you will find as many religions as books, and for this plain reason each makes his own experience the standard of religion." –Laurence W. Wood, *Theology as History and Hermeneutics*, and Diane Leclerc, *Discovering Christian Holiness*

How firm a foundation, you saints of the Lord,
Is laid for your faith in God's excellent Word!
What more can be said than to you God hath said,
to you who for refuge to Jesus have fled? . . . (George Keith?)

Holy Bible, book divine,
precious treasure, thou art mine . . . (John Burton Sr.)

O, send Thy Spirit, Lord, now unto me,
that He may touch my eyes and make me see;

Show me the truth concealed within Thy word,
for in Thy book revealed, I see Thee, Lord . . . (Alexander Groves)

'Tis so sweet to trust in Jesus,
and to take him and his word;
Just to rest upon his promise,
and to know, "Thus saith the Lord" . . . (Louisa Stead)

Unlock the truth, Thyself the key,
Unseal the sacred book . . . (Charles Wesley)

Sing them over again to me,
wonderful words of life;
Let me more of their beauty see,
wonderful words of life . . . (Philip P. Bliss)

Silently now I wait for Thee,
ready my God Thy will to see;
Open my heart, illumine me,
Spirit divine! . . . (Clara Scott)

We praise Thee for the radiance
that from the hallowed page,
a lantern to our footsteps,
shines on from age to age . . . (William Walsham How)

Standing on the promises that cannot fail,
when the howling storms of doubt and fear assail;
by the living Word of God, I shall prevail,
standing on the promises of God . . . (R. Kelso Carter)

Beyond the sacred page,
I seek Thee, Lord;
my spirit pants for Thee,
O Living Word! . . . (Mary A. Lathbury)

SOME NUGGETS ARE ESSENTIAL ROCKS

GOD, THE ROCK

The Rock, his work is perfect, and all his ways are just.
(Deut. 32:4)

There is no holy one like the Lord, No one besides you; There is no rock like our God.
(1 Sam. 2:2)

Listen to me, You who pursue righteousness, you who seek the Lord. Look to the Rock from which you were hewn. And to the quarry from which you were dug.
(Isa. 51:1)

The Lord is my Rock, my fortress, and my deliverer, my God, my Rock in whom I take refuge.
(Ps. 18:2)

The Truths of God
For the People of God

Happy are those whose delight is in the law of the Lord, and on his law they meditate day and night. . . . The unfolding of your words gives light; it imparts understanding to the simple. . . . I remember the days of old; I think about all your deeds; my soul thirsts for you. (Ps. 1:1-2; 119:130; 143:5-6)

They devoted themselves to the apostles' teaching and fellowship. . . . Go, therefore, and make disciples of all nations, teaching them to obey everything that I have commanded you. (Acts 2:42; Matt. 28:19-20)

IV

The Thought that Helpfully Conveys

A "theologian" is a believer seeking to think carefully about the things of God. Thinking wisely and then organizing our best thoughts is a worthy Christian venture always essential but never finished. All believers should be theologians, at least in an informal sense. We recommend rejoicing in the golden nuggets clustering around the center of Christian truth rather than picking and judging around the edges. We choose not to attempt preparing for the reader a prepackaged systematic theology. We focus rather on highlighting foundational building blocks.

Following are twenty-nine golden nuggets of Christian truth, orienting thoughts to guide the believer on safe and productive paths of theological thought. We do this with confidence and humility, gladly confessing that "we see through a glass darkly." Our thoughts are limited frameworks for grappling with a more complex reality than our theories can capture. We must meet and trust the Person who is Himself the Truth. An educated person and a mature disciple is one who believes while not being sure, is passionate and yet open-minded, and takes a position but listens to other people with humility. See V. James Mannoia Jr., *Paradox and Virtue*.

Glimpses of the following Golden Nuggets

1. To really believe is to put your entire life on the line.
2. Theology is the church trying to understand itself.
3. There's just too much nonsense in the theological world!

4. Good theology must go beyond the mind, clear to the soul.
5. The best theologians should be mentors, not masters.
6. God always will be a mystery to be approached with awe.
7. No theology is final, but must make sense to the hearers.
8. Many of great early theologians were Africans?
9. Activate your whole brain to get theology right.
10. We're in need of the Spirit's help to think well.
11. Use freedom and be careful with disjunctive pairs.
12. God's grace comes through the cracks in our human jars.
13. Good theology includes thinking, singing, even dancing!
14. Authority is multiple, the Bible aided in three ways.
15. Adapt Jesus to the world's thinking, but not too much!
16. Bad theology gives false reasons for human suffering.
17. Focus on the central truths: Cross and Resurrection.
18. Take into account that God appears to prefer the poor.
19. Change your mind. Nobody gets theology all right.
20. Use your creed as a tool, not a club.
21. "Liberal arts" are really essential.
22. Material things stimulate insight and good theology.
23. Doubt even your doubts—they could be wrong.
24. It's important to begin with "apostolic" doctrine.
25. When doing theology, better to go to the East or the West?
26. Don't parade half of a truth as the whole, that's "heresy"!
27. Theology should be humble, not gate keeping.
28. Try to stay clear of the devil's tricky definitions.
29. Religion can be a dangerous place to live!

1. *CREDO*: I BELIEVE

Christians who first said *credo* ("I believe") did not do so lightly, but at the risk of their lives under severe persecution. We listen carefully to those who are prepared to sacrifice their lives for their belief. To say *credo* genuinely is to speak from the heart, to reveal who one is by confessing one's essential belief, the faith that makes life worth living, even giving up if necessary. One who says *credo* without willingness to suffer, and if necessary die, for the faith has not yet genuinely said *credo*.

Christians have a right and responsibility to know the meaning of their baptism. This is the purpose of Christian theology, to clarify the ancient faith into which Christians of all times and places are baptized. It is expected of all believers that they come to understand what it means to believe in God the Father Almighty, in God the Son, and in God the Spirit. The meaning didn't originate in the word processor of an ancient Greek theologian but in the life experience of ordinary people who knew Jesus and his Spirit and found something happening in their lives that had never happened before.
–Thomas C. Oden, *Classic Christianity,* and Frederick Buechner, *Beyond Words*

2. FAITH'S STORY FOR AND WITH OTHERS

Christian theology is a careful articulation of the story of the church, the nature of its present liberty, and the vitality of its hope for those within and beyond the community of faith. Theology is undertaken on behalf of the church to bring clarity and understanding of its own witness. It also is done for the sake of the other. The church must not simply talk to itself, engaging in uninterrupted monologues. The theological task considers the "other," those for whom Christ died but who have not yet found an abundance of grace upon grace. This aspect of the task gives the church a public voice as theologians currently dialoging with various intellectual currents, not all of which are open to the prospects of faith.

Even with the best of intentions, there likely is no such thing as disinterested or unbiased theologizing. Christian theology is *human speech* about God. For instance, Afro-Pentecostal voices finally are now speaking out about the particularities of their distinctive experience of biblical interpretation and context, but they also are limited in these regards. Aren't we all? We should be open and humble. The theological undertaking must include dialogue with church and academy, Pentecostals and all other believers. "Establishment" voices must be aware that the oppressed also have something of importance to say. –Kenneth J. Collins, *The Evangelical Moment,* and Ivan Hartsfield, *Sanctified Imagination*

3. LET'S SKIP THE NONSENSE

A simple preacher from the Ozarks served as the first president of Anderson University. Here's his thinking. Faith without reason is an ally of theological dogmatism and religious superstition, bosom friends of error. But reason without faith is a half-blind rationalism which assumes all reality must be logically verified, an assumption which itself is unreasonable. The universe is so full of mystery that human reason alone is a puny instrument for reaching the fullness of truth. Faith and reason are like the light and heat of the sun. They cannot be separated. To put one against the other is nonsense.

Maybe that's why much theology that people have heard about makes no sense to them. It really is nonsense! We who do theology are tempted to parade our most complex thinking as ultimate truth when our minds aren't equipped to comprehend and articulate the fullness of God's reality. Good theology must be both a medium of God's voice and an admission of our quite humble efforts to receive and convey that voice. –Barry L. Callen, *The Wisdom of the Saints*

4. NOT OF THE TONGUE ONLY

True Christian doctrine is not a matter for the tongue, but of life, and not grasped only by the intellect as is true in some other fields of study. Rather, doctrine is rightly received only when it takes possession of the soul and finds a dwelling place in the most intimate affections of the heart. John Calvin's highly developed systematic theology needs adjusted by a greater appreciation of the countering emphases of the eighteenth-century reformer John Wesley. Although agreeing on many aspects of theology, there is significant difference between these two reformers in their understandings of God and how God works in this fallen world.

Calvin's theological strength is also his greatest weakness. Christian life is not something best described as a "system"—a logically constructed interconnection of beliefs and values. Such a description is more applicable to rationalist philosophy or Christian scholasticism than to the Bible and actual life. Whereas "systematic" theology is rationally appealing in Western societies, Wesley's more practically oriented approach to theology is more appropriate and reflective of biblical revelation. Especially is this true when it comes to describing the dynamics of life in the Spirit of God. –Don Thorsen, *Calvin vs Wesley*

5. MENTORS BUT NOT GURUS

We Christian theologians are to learn from great Christian thinkers of the past without becoming slaves to their precise conclusions. Martin Luther and John Calvin had the task of defining their reforming movements in the face of hostile governments. John Wesley profited from them but had the rather different task in England of finding ways to allow the vibrant Word of God to vitalize cold even if correct theological traditions. Martin, John, and John now all are valuable mentors for us, mentors but *not gurus*. The guru is a master to be followed, obeyed, and imitated. Wesley himself was deeply indebted to history. History, however, did not throttle him. He caught the torch from those before him and flung it out for others to carry and refine.

Christian holiness is the vitalizing spiritual energy that renews the churches through spiritually renewed people. Such people are gifted by the Spirit to be God's rethinking and reforming disciples, enabled by yesterday's mentors while not being paralyzed by gurus of any time. The Holy Spirit has given the church an abundance of gifts for her sustenance and healing. What matters most is our reception of the Giver of the gifts, the life-giving Holy Spirit who comes to baptize and immerse us into the life of God. –Mildred Bangs Wynkoop, in *Wesleyan Theological Society*, and William (Billy) Abraham, *Canon and Criterion*

6. THE MUDDY WORLD OF HERESY

Christian faith doesn't try to solve the mysteriousness of all mysteries. We're dealing with God, not math problems that have very clear answers. Solving the divine mysteries with mental simplicities that we can fully comprehend is to fall into the muddy world of heresy. Encountering the mystery of God is to humbly glimpse and be in touch with ultimate truth itself. Rather than providing all answers, perceiving God through Jesus Christ at least presents the proper angle of view and spawns exhilaration and wonder and joy.

Wisdom lies in not trying to fully explain, the inclination of the Western church. It's better to be satisfied with embracing the mystery in reverence, awe, and delight, the focus of the Eastern church. When we have finished our theologizing, we must admit that we will not understand all mysteries. We are human pilgrims following the pathways of knowledge. To the end of the earthly way, we shall still know only in part. Even so, our faith in Jesus Christ, our Lord, can give us the assurance of things hoped for and the conviction of things not seen. –Georgia E. Harkness, *Understanding the Christian Faith*

7. THINGS PUT IN CONTEXT

The gospel of Christ is for all people and must be contextualized. Relevancy is an inherent quality of the kingdom of God. It must be effective in any context where it's proclaimed. Otherwise, the result is isolation, sectarianism, and irrelevancy, common plagues infecting Christian life. The Kingdom message is meant to meet people where they are and give them the hope of grace that comes from God. Doing the work of Christian theology is seeking to contextualize our thinking about and witnessing for God. The language and thought patterns used must be understood and the particular social setting addressed. Since cultures are constantly changing, the work of theology is never done.

We must get beyond the temptation of believing that our way of putting things is final for all people in all times and places. We must be about the task of doing Christian theology modestly as well as faithfully and constantly. For example, the church today needs a restating and living out of the doctrine of Christian holiness in all its dimensions—personal, relational, social, and political—in the context of our cultures and in the idioms of our time. We must learn to prize such diversity of experience and expression and speak to it in accord with biblical revelation. –Kevin W. Mannoia, *Church 2K*, and Roger Green in *The Holiness Manifesto*

8. OUR AFRICAN BEGINNINGS

Speaking of cultural context, did you know that the earliest forms of classic Christian teaching bear a distinctly African stamp? Christian intellectual formation is oldest in Africa. The contributions made by African Christian thinkers had decisive effects on the formation of world Christianity, especially European. African Christianity is foundational for classic Christian teaching. Unfortunately, racial and national prejudices run deep. They are so hurtful and blind. Modern Americans think all is new and better than ever. Not so, at least not with Christian faith.

You may not know these African names but their wisdom radiates through much of Christian teaching across the centuries--Tertullian, Origen, Cyprian, Athanasius, Didymus the Blind, Augustine, and the great Cyril. Christianity often is portrayed as an essentially European religion. This is regrettable because classic Christianity has its pre-European roots in cultures that are far distant from Europe. Some of the greatest Christian minds have been African. We must contextualize the teachings of Christ to fit the times, yes, but only as the enduring raw materials of revealed truth are being honored. –Thomas C. Oden, *Classic Christianity*

9. RIGHT-BRAINED AND LEFT-BRAINED

Theology often tends to either/or ways of thinking and fails to grasp the breadth and depth of the biblical gospel. This is particularly true of highly rationalistic forms of theology, including much of contemporary Evangelicalism. One great strength of John Wesley's thought and practice is its inclusive, both/and character. This is seen in his affirmation of both God's sovereignty and human freedom, salvation by faith and the necessity of good works, and the continuing value of the Law despite the priority of grace. He was both rational and poetic, right-brained and left-brained. He lived at the height of the Age of Reason and at the beginning of the new interest in human experience, emotion, and relations.

The "conjunctive" nature of Wesley's theology runs deep. God's truth is so grand that it readily transcends our rational tools and categories. Still, it is fundamentally reasonable while being fundamentally personal. Our theological dialogue must include many voices, past and present, global and local, West and East, and move across cultures in an ongoing engagement between Scripture and contextual challenges. God is still up to something through Jesus Christ by the Spirit, and it's exciting to be part of it! –Howard S. Snyder, in *Wesleyan Theological Society*

10. GOD GIVES PEOPLE FREEDOM

Both John Wesley and John Calvin believed in the sovereignty, power, and majesty of God. The difference is that Calvin thought such beliefs resulted in divine control of all that happens while Wesley thought that, in love and through undeserved grace, God chooses to enable people to exercise freedom and accept or reject God's salvation. Wesley thought Calvin was mistaken to believe that God's sovereignty overwhelms the freedom of people, making it negligible or even non-existent.

Most Christians believe that God is sovereign and that they have a significant amount of freedom regarding their salvation and for day-to-day decisions. Their sense of freedom to make significant decisions for this life and their eternal life is not illusory. Their decision-making ability is made possible by God's grace. We rightly give praise and thanks for God's Spirit for aiding us in all that happens. Because of this grace-enabled liberty, Christians can love as they are loved by God. In biblical words, "We love because he first loved us" (1 Jn. 4:19). –Don Thorsen, *Calvin vs Wesley*

11. A COMPREHENSIVE VISION

John Wesley's orienting concern, "responsible grace," bridges longstanding theological divides. It avoids any merited salvation while upholding the importance of our transformation into Christlikeness. This orienting concern can stress God's gracious sovereignty in a way that actually enhances the place of human responsiveness. It's a conception that can illuminate the vital connections between the pardoning and transforming dimensions of divine grace. It can value the many means through which grace is mediated without rendering use of these means mechanical or presumptuous.

Wesley's theological significance for today rests on his ability to integrate contrasting emphases vital to a healthy and comprehensive vision of the Christian faith. Consider these disjunctive pairs: faith, works; personal devotions, sacramental practice; personal piety, social concern; justification, sanctification; evangelism, Christian nurture; Bible, tradition; revelation, reason; commitment, civility; creation, redemption; cell group, institutional church; local scene, world parish. Carefully merging these pairs, Wesley deserves to be read and pondered yet today. –Randy L. Maddox, *Responsible Grace,* and William (Billy) J. Abraham, *The Coming Great Revival*

12. GRACE THROUGH THE JAR'S CRACKS

One recounting of a personal spiritual odyssey comes to a wise conclusion. Are you disillusioned with the church, its leadership, and even the Christian faith itself? If so, you are not alone. Every generation experiences such disappointment. I know because I have been in the depths of disillusionment myself. Yet the church continues. Leaders lead and faith somehow persists. Why? Because God has given us the gift of divine grace in *jars of clay* to show that the "all-surpassing power is from God and not of us." It's through the cracks in our human jars that we get glimpses of God at work in astounding ways.

My personal story (David McKenna) is one of growing up under the demands of an autocratic leader in a holiness tabernacle. The jars of clay, both individual and institutional, were obvious. So were the cracks in the clay. Through those very cracks we see the harsh reality of human nature exercising its might in contest with the all-surpassing power of God. We also get glimpses of God's grace at work. I only ask that you be open to the evidence that grace upon grace is at work to redeem us and make us whole. Good theology consists of good glimpses through the cracks. –David L. McKenna, *The Triumphs of His Grace*

13. A HEALTHY COMBINATION

Charles Wesley too often is placed in the background of his famous brother John. Both lived in the religious awakening of the eighteenth century and were major contributors to it. Charles was a chronicler and hymnist of the awakening. He brought to his time and still to ours a healthy combination that provides strength and depth to Christian theology. Charles embodied and sang the tension between the free spirit of the Evangelical Revival and the liturgical traditions of the English church. To the free spirit, he brought biblical and theological order. To the liturgic tradition he brought the "dancing heart."

Music is central to Christian worship and even evangelism. We humans are thinkers and feelers. If John was more the formal thinker, his brother Charles was the one who could set hearts ablaze with verse and rhythm. Mused one establishment churchman of their time, "For one who has been drawn away by doctrine, ten have been induced by music." Charles wedded great thoughts to powerful sounds that thrill the heart." What Christian doesn't know "Hark! The Herald Angels Sing," "O, for a Thousand Tongues to Sing," and "Christ the Lord is Risen Today!" Good theology involves thinking carefully and feeling deeply. John Wesley once advised, "Beware of singing as if you were half dead or half asleep, but lift up your voice with strength." –T. Crichton Mitchell, *Charles Wesley: Man with the Dancing Heart*

14. THE WESLEYAN QUADRILATERAL

The *Wesleyan Quadrilateral* is a shorthand way that many of today's followers of John Wesley use to summarize Christian religious authority. This fourfold understanding includes *Scripture, tradition, reason*, and *experience*. Wesley considered Scripture to be unique, inspired, trustworthy, and the primary religious authority for Christian beliefs, values, and practices. In addition, he appealed to tradition, reason, and experience as genuine even if secondary religious authorities that help Christians contextualize their understanding and application of biblical Christianity.

It's important to investigate the full range of religious data and ways of understanding it best. An analogy helps one understand the integrative character of this quadrilateral. Scripture, tradition, reason, and experience function as an organic whole in the search to understand and apply best the revealed truth of God. Scripture serves as the head, but we should not speak of a single part of the body without reference to the wisdom contributions of the others. The various parts of the body are necessarily interdependent and crucial to each other in understanding the function of the whole. –Don Thorsen, *The Wesleyan Quadrilateral*

15. ADAPT, BUT NOT TOO MUCH!

Today's world of diversities tempts the Christian to place Jesus into the melting pot of the world's religions, only one of the bright lights of truth available for humans to follow. The claim of Jesus, however, is that he is *the truth*. To back away from this is to back up too far. Even so, this absolute claim must be held with humility. God in Jesus for our salvation is the supreme truth about reality at its highest. And yet, God is everywhere active, we might say Jesus in disguise, the Spirit of Jesus permeating other religious traditions with hints of the ultimate. Truth is where you find it. Respect for others is essential. Christian systems of theology, ethics, and organizations are not themselves part of the absolute claim, only Jesus.

Good theology in some ways should always be changing. The process is one of moving between two poles, the Bible as the primary source of theological truth and the present culture as the source of mental categories in which the truth must now be expressed so that the truth of Christ can be understood. Scripture remains the norm for theological statements. Nevertheless, effective communication demands that the theologian take seriously the thought forms and mindset of the culture of the present time and place. –Stanley J. Grenz, *Revisioning Evangelical Theology*

16. FOUR BAD ASSUMPTIONS

Job had his unexplained suffering and his supporting friends who were poor theologians trying to help. Their assumption was that the person who lives a good life in obedience to God will be rewarded with good fortune, health, wealth, and happiness. Choosing to live otherwise will be punished accordingly. It turns out that few things are as dangerous as semi-truths. Here are four common assumptions that are slightly right and dangerously wrong, leading to defective although popular theology. *All suffering comes from God.* God is sovereign, so our lives surely are pre-planned in detail and always go as planned. The response to this should be yes and no. Then *all suffering must be caused by the sin of the sufferer*? We certainly do bring much harm to ourselves, but the response to this still is to be yes and no.

Then is *all suffering completely random*? Yes and no. Buddhists claim that *suffering is an unnecessary illusion.* Extinguish desire for transitory things and suffering will go away. They have a point, but again an inadequate one. Job never got a direct answer from God about the cause of his suffering other than that God is God and all answers to life's dilemmas aren't available right now to mere humans. Job had to become comfortable with *not knowing the unknowable.* Such humility is a good way to begin doing Christian theology. –Barry L. Callen, *The Jagged Journey*

17. FOCUS ON THE CENTRAL TRUTHS

A central truth of Christian theology is about the particular kind of strength that characterizes God. God created humans with the ability to choose the intended good. The great love of God accepts our decisions and is open to participating constructively in the suffering created by the evil of our wrong choices. Our suffering must be viewed in light of God's great love and voluntary vulnerability on our behalf. Our ability to choose is a gift of God, a "risk" God has willingly and lovingly taken. This divine love and vulnerability are seen most clearly in a barn near Bethlehem and on a cross near Jerusalem.

The resurrection of Jesus makes plain that God was *with us* and *for us* as the Son murdered on the cross. Mystery remains, yes, but what we do know is that darkness has been overwhelmed by light. Given the resurrection of Jesus, even the cross glows with glory! The heart of biblical revelation is this. God in Christ has identified personally with our suffering. The main answer to the problem of our pain is the pain of God. God voluntarily has participated in our suffering, the innocent for the guilty. Why? In order that the pain of our guilt could be purged of divine judgment and cleansed of any continuing power over our existence and destiny. That's the heart of all good Christian theology. –Barry L. Callen, *The Jagged Journey*

18. A PREFERENCE IN GOD'S MERCY

One of the more important themes of contemporary theology is the claim that God's mercy contains an element of "divine partiality." God's love is focused particularly on "a preferential option for the poor," a key dimension of the biblical witness which must find expression in the life of the church. We are to pay close attention to Jesus when he summarizes the goals of his own ministry. They were "to preach good news to the poor, to proclaim release to the captives and recovery of sight to the blind, to set free those who are oppressed" (Lk. 4:18-19).

This preference for ministry focus is a defining characteristic of the church's intended being and mission yet today. Holiness people used to "dress down," not just to protest shameful cultural patterns and preserve personal modesty, but to welcome the poor by allowing them to feel comfortable around church people. We dare not suppress this ministry focus, including the oppression of women in Christian leadership. B. T. Roberts was right. Can the church get along without a bishop? Maybe. However, there can be no church without a gospel, and one including a gospel for the poor. –Donald W. Dayton, in the *Wesleyan Theological Journal* (1991)

19. DARE TO CHANGE WHEN NECESSARY

What about changing one's mind in theology? Is it acceptable to explore and experiment with theological frontiers? There must be a constancy of direction and intent. That's toward a renewed spiritual identity that enlivens a biblically defined faith concerned with Christ's mission. There also must be a continued respect for Christianity's traditional authority sources, but without being victimized by any classic theorizing about them. Change there must be, but change consistent with the whole biblical witness and the present work of God's Spirit.

There always is more to be learned. Rather than being known only as one who has the courage of his convictions, it would be good also to be known as one who has the courage to question and change old opinions when they need changing. We learn best as we remain open in the Spirit and engage in honest dialogue with the larger believing community. This is what it means to be "catholic" in conviction and learning. Jesus assured faithful disciples that his Spirit would be with believers forever, guiding them into all the truth. –Barry L. Callen, *Journey Toward Renewal*

20. CREEDS AS TOOLS, NOT CLUBS

Christian creeds formulate truth in verbal packages, but there's always a degree of inadequacy to these packages. A life hidden with God could be likened to falling in love. Theological statements come along to package understandings of this love. However, an essay on love and actually being in love *are not the same thing*. Believing rightly about God is essential, of course. Being in a love relationship with God is more foundational than a few faltering words trying to describe adequately the experience. There's a world of difference between learning to repeat "God is an omnipotent being" and addressing God directly with, "Thou art *my* God!"

Christian faith doesn't begin with a thesis discovered in the mind but with a love relationship initiated by God. Believers should seek to love the Lord and put that life-transforming experience into words the best way they can for the understanding of others. They should seek forgiveness when getting arrogant and insisting that others word their beliefs in exactly the same way. We should focus more on the love relationships and less on frail theological formalities. We should use our creeds as constructive means of sharing and not as clubs to gain dominance of our own thinking. –Barry L. Callen, *Caught Between Truths*

21. SPOTTING THE ULTIMATE IN WISDOM

There are two kinds of education, one preparing you to make a living and another preparing you to know how to live. There is a new generation of thinkers now willing to work with appreciation about the latter kind of education, seeking life's wisdom in wonder, meditation, experience, beauty, intuition, and love. They are ready to add to their telescopes and computers and big data bases an embracing of the faith dimension of life's fuller understanding. Maybe, after all, there is meaningfulness and deep insight in spiritual experience and divine revelation.

Despite all the "information" now at hand, are we yet humble enough to listen carefully to Jesus as he invites the children to his feet? There is the serious possibility that the kingdom of God, the ultimate in wisdom, might be somewhat childlike. We applaud those Christian universities that still insist on the "liberal arts" for all students regardless of their professional goals. Young humans need "liberated" to the breadth and depth dimensions of truth and life, not just equipped to do some money-gaining job. After all, Christian theology once was known as the "Queen of the Sciences." –Kevin W. Mannoia, *Expressing Life*

22. EXCITED ABOUT GREEK LANGUAGE AND ICONS?

The Greek word *ginosko* means "to know." When you put the prefix *epi* in front, it gets intensified into *really knowing*. That's what we want, to truly perceive, to know intimately, not just intellectually but in a way that alters life itself. The two men on their way to Emmaus met and talked with the resurrected Jesus. It was only surface awareness, a casual chat with a stranger. Then over a meal "their eyes were opened and they recognized him" (Lk. 24:31). They moved from knowing to *really knowing*. Faith has eyes that see beyond the obvious and immediate.

The theological works of men like John Wesley and Clark Pinnock are quite nuanced and yet not designed for intellectual elites.

These were "practical" theologians deeply concerned about church renewal, partly through the established "means of grace," and sometimes by unexpected manifestations of God's Spirit. The Spirit can render common material things agents of spiritual insight and growth. Some means are common, like the Lord Supper and Baptism. Others just happen as individuals are open to the Spirit's presence always revealing divine grace to us. Material carriers of the Spirit's truth and life are called "icons." Have there been any in your life recently? Stroke a baby, see a sunset, feed the hungry, inhale the fragrance of a flower and be touched by God. –Barry L. Callen, *Approaching Theology*

23. LET'S DOUBT OUR DOUBTS

Faith is the victory that overcomes the world, so we tend to say that doubt is faith's chief enemy. Still, all of us who believe have experienced times of doubt unless we live in a state of denial or thoughtless void. Faith can falter when suffering surges. We all have a stake in that ancient prayer, "Lord I believe, help my unbelief" (Mk. 9:24). A real advance in the life of faith awaits believers in God when they finally develop a more realistic and wholesome attitude toward doubt. There may be more genuine faith in honest doubt than in the blind believing of some conventional creed. Doubt keeps faith awake and moving. It isn't the opposite of faith; it's an element of it.

We should dare to doubt even our doubts. When your world goes wrong, don't feel sorry for yourself. Plunge more deeply into the jagged journey of faith, believing that God waits along the way with healing in his wings. Paul told the Roman Christians that there was no safe place to hide. Instead of hiding, we should "Wake up from our slumber. The night is nearly over. Clothe yourselves with the Lord Jesus Christ" (Rom. 11:14). The great word of faith is "nevertheless!" Our generalizations can get contradicted and our dogmas dynamited. Still, these disruptions don't deserve the last word. Beyond them should come the persistent faith assertion, nevertheless! –Frederick Buechner, *Beyond Words*

24. NEVER NEGLECT APOSTOLIC DOCTRINE

At least one thing Christian believers should not allow themselves to doubt is the necessity of Christian doctrine being both understood and activated. Learning to express and share core Christian beliefs are necessary mission tasks. They should not be abandoned no matter how frustrating they might be at times. The earliest fellowships of believers devoted themselves to what Jesus and his first apostles taught. They have sought increasingly to understand this "apostolic" teaching. God has not communicated a system of dogma involving finished statements about the whole scope of Christian truth that just needs to be memorized. We must go back and then go on.

Theology, disciplined thinking about God, shouldn't consist only of popular concepts from human culture. Early believers studied the "apostles' doctrine" (Acts 2:42), attempting to teach what Jesus himself taught (Matt. 28:20). The church is to be a place of this intentional theological learning and sharing. Otherwise, it ceases to be the church. When apostolic doctrine is neglected, personal opinion takes precedence over biblical truths, ethics become situational, cultural notions replace vital orthodoxy, and emotion becomes a primary concern and controlling force. –James Earl Massey, *Views from the Mountain,* and H. Ray Dunning, *Grace, Faith, & Holiness*

25. THEOLOGY AS MORE AWE OR ANALYSIS?

The Great Schism of 1054 divided the Western and Eastern worlds of Christianity. The great mysteries of the faith, like the doctrine of God, are approached rather differently in these divided worlds. The West, Roman Catholicism and most of Protestantism, tends toward *analysis* while the East favors *adoration*. There are major Western "systematic" theologies by Aquinas, Calvin, Barth, and others. Nothing like this is found in the East. Christian leaders there are more comfortable in merging reason and experience, theology and spirituality, cognition without wanting to resolve mystery.

John Wesley is something of a Western exception. Rather than speculating at length about complex philosophic concepts, he joins the East in focusing on holiness, theological understanding resting on communing with the living God. Especially with his brother

Charles, the great hymn writer, John recognized the value of music and community dynamics in the quest for truth and mature faith. Aesthetic images and testimonies of spiritual experience are highlighted in addition to classic documents and complex arguments.
–Daniel B. Clendenin, *Eastern Orthodox Christianity*

26. BEING CAUGHT IN BETWEEN

Christians are caught between two unyielding facts when seeking to share their faith with non-believers. We must be true to the historic foundations of the faith and also sensitive to what it will take to communicate that faith effectively to modern hearers. To fail in the first is to have the wrong message; to fail in the second is to have the right message which is not being heard or really understood. Witnessing to our faith is not an either/or business.

Most theological "heresies" in the past haven't been someone teaching an outright falsehood. They have been parading half of a truth and insisting that it's the whole thing. Was Jesus really God with us or truly a human? The "orthodox" (proper thinking) answer is "Yes!" Is the Bible a human production or truly God's Word? "Yes!" Are humans the crown of God's creation or its biggest crisis? "Yes!" Is the church the pure Bride of Christ or congregations of frail humans only on their way to becoming "saints"? "Yes!" Is one part of any such pairings, when separated from the other, the truth? No! –Barry L. Callen, *Caught Between Truths*

27. THEOLOGY AS A TENTATIVE JOURNEY

Responsible faith always asks questions. Christian theology is done best when the community of faith takes real interest in the truth and knows that it is not enough to merely repeat traditional foundations of doctrine. Believers must persist in searching for the truth to which the traditions point, but which they only partially express. I've been a theological pilgrim (Clark Pinnock). Theology for me has been a journey of discovery, so I have respected but have not regarded traditional views as beyond reform. Our theology is a work of human construction, even when based on divine revelation. Interpretation of that revelation requires strenuous effort. I engage in open-ended thinking, offering tentative solutions. I welcome diversity of opinion and look to others to help me build on insights of the past.

I have found that one cannot engage in the task of reforming traditional thought and escape criticism. It would be helpful if we could discuss very important matters as seekers after truth rather than as stubborn gate keepers obsessed by who is in and who is out of the true evangelical movement. I recognize the inadequacy of my mind to comprehend God, and therefore I understand why I am viewed in certain quarters as a danger to sound theology. Those who are absolutely sure of their belief conclusions and are not open to any alternative considerations naturally are uncomfortable with me in the room. So be it. I journey on. –Clark H. Pinnock, *Most Moved Mover*

28. CAREFUL OF THE DEVIL'S DEFINITIONS

In *The Devil's Dictionary* we find satirical definitions like this. "Indigestion" is sometimes mistaken for deep religious conviction. A Native American is supposed to have said, "Plenty well, no pray; big bellyache, heap God!" Yes, we humans all have failing bodies with swirling emotions and unanswered questions, and we do tend to turn to God only when in a heap of trouble. The question is, when our digestive system has cleared, is God still there? Be careful of the definitions of the Devil!

A prominent teacher of mine announced that he "hated fog, especially when it's inside the heads of my students!" The class was encouraged to participate only after having thought carefully so that the fog had cleared. There was an awkward silence in the room. Theology has its lingering fog, continuing the need for faith, ongoing theological work, and caution about rash speaking. What about the Devil defining *religion* as "a daughter of hope and fear, explaining to ignorance the nature of the unknowable." Is belief in God really that self-serving and impossible? Is Christian theology so sophisticated an endeavor that even God might fail an exam about himself? –Barry L. Callen, *Approaching Theology* and *The Heart of the Matter*

29. LIVING HUMBLY IN THE PRESENCE (GOD)

We see in the Old Testament prophets like Amos that religion can go very wrong, turn in on itself, say all the right things and still be a mockery in God's eyes. Religion is one of the surest ways to avoid faith in the real and present God. That was demonstrated in the New Testament by the murder of Jesus. Who killed him? It was the priests and theologians. The ones who accepted him were the lepers, drunkards, and prostitutes. Truth isn't always where we suppose. As Jesus says, be prepared for the surprise that "the first will be last, and the last will be first" (Matt. 19:30).

We must let go of three primary things. First is the compulsion to be successful. Second is the compulsion to be right, especially to be theologically right. Finally, there is the compulsion to be powerful, to have everything under control. I am convinced that these are the three demons Jesus faced in the wilderness. So long as we haven't looked these demons in the face, we should presume that they are still in charge. How different things are when we consciously are living humbly in *the Presence* (God), with truth filling our awareness and yet beyond our comprehension. –Richard Rohr, *What the Mystics Know*

From the hymnbook of the Hebrews (Psalms):
    The enduring love of God, Ps. 136:1–3
    How God reveals himself in creation, Ps. 136:4–9
    How God revealed himself in Israel's history, Ps. 136: 10–26

From the New Testament (1 Tim. 3:16+)
    The mystery of godliness:
        He was manifested in the flesh,
        vindicated by the Spirit,
        seen by angels, proclaimed among the nations,
        believed on in the world, and taken up in glory.

There should be no artificial distinction between "objective" theology and personal spiritual experience of that theology. The 1780 Hymnbook, for instance, is structured, not by the categories of systematic theology, but as a "Methodist Pilgrim's Progress."

More about Jesus, let me learn,
More of his holy will discern;
Spirit of God, my teacher be,
Showing the things of Christ to me . . . (Eliza E. Hewitt)

In that land of perfect day, when the mists have rolled away,
We will understand it better by and by . . . (Charles A. Tindley)

Be still, my soul; your God will undertake
to guide the future as he has the past;
Your hope, your confidence, let nothing shake;
all now mysterious shall be bright at last . . .
(Kathrina von Schlegel)

I sing the wisdom that ordained the sun to rule the day.
The moon shines full at his command,
and all the stars obey . . . (Isaac Watts)

With my mouth will I make known
Thy faithfulness, Thy faithfulness.
With my mouth will I make known
Thy faithfulness to all generations . . . (James H. Fillmore)

SOME NUGGETS ARE ESSENTIAL ROCKS

JESUS, THE CORNERSTONE

The Lord says, I lay a stone in Zion, a tested stone, a precious cornerstone for a sure foundation. The one who trusts will never be dismayed. I will make justice the measuring line and righteousness the plumb line.

(Isa. 28: 16-17)

Come to him, a living stone, though rejected by mortals, yet chosen and precious in God's sight. And like living stones, let yourselves be built into a spiritual house, to be a holy priesthood, to offer spiritual sacrifices acceptable to God through Jesus Christ.

(1 Pet. 2:4-5)

The Truths of God
For the People of God

God chose us in Christ before the foundation of the world to be holy and blameless before him in love. . . . We are to be like living stones, built into a spiritual house to be a holy priesthood, to offer spiritual sacrifices acceptable to God . . . . I am confident that the one who began a good work in you will continue to complete it. (Eph. 1:4; 1 Pet. 2:5; Phil. 1:6)

Now that you have been freed from sin and enslaved to God, the fruit you have leads to sanctification, and the end is eternal life. . . . Let us cleanse ourselves from every defilement of flesh and spirit, making holiness perfect in the fear of God. (Rom. 6:22; 2 Cor. 7:1)

V

The Experience that Truly Transforms

God's people are supposed to think and act like God, actually representing God to the world. Being "holy" as God is holy surely is a God-sized challenge for human-sized believers. Is it possible? John Calvin and John Wesley may have differed on some things, but both insisted on the need for Christian "holiness." None have rightly learned Christ who have not learned that they must put off the "old man" and "put on Christ." We are to be children of God who bear the marks of the divine family. God our Father calls us to be clothed in the Son.

Paul addressed the membership of the church in Corinth as those "who are sanctified in Christ Jesus, called to be saints" (1 Cor. 1:2). A Christian "saint" isn't a marble statue of spiritual perfection but a humble believer who has experienced a transformation of the inner nature by the gracious work of the Spirit. Being "saved" means more than being rendered guiltless of past sin. It includes becoming different, being transformed by divine grace into increasing Christlikeness. Following are nineteen golden nuggets of Christian truth about this glorious transformation goal and process. The first two raise concern about the direction we are headed.

Glimpses of the following Golden Nuggets

1. The consumerist culture has put holes in our holiness message.
2. The nation and churches are off course.

3. "Holiness" is the central aspect of God's very nature.
4. "Pentecostal spirituality" is the kingdom filled with passion.
5. Christian congregations should be holiness training schools.
6. The Holy Spirit enables life in accord with the life of God.
7. The cross-centered love of God is perfected in weakness.
8. If any church offers discount coupons, it's fraudulent.
9. God came in Christ and still comes in the Spirit for us.
10. The Spirit is a foretaste of coming eternal newness.
11. The Holy Spirit was once *experience* more than *doctrine*.
12. Jesus points to a cross to get to resurrection.
13. God's way is the uniting fire of the Spirit's cleansing.
14. Christian holiness is like flying around a barn.
15. We learn that the evil snake has its head cut off!
16. What does being "saved" really mean?
17. Is the church really any different than the world?
18. Listen to the sounds in the silence.
19. Is the best prayer with your mouth or your life?
20. Stand up in praise to God!

1. A HOLE IN OUR HOLINESS

The hole in the quest for Christian holiness is that many of us don't care that much about it. It's not that we don't talk about sin or encourage decent behavior. It's that too many sermons are basically self-help seminars on becoming a better you. Any gospel which says only what you must do and never announces what Christ *has done* is no gospel at all. We face the failure of Christians to take seriously one of the great aims of our redemption and one of the required evidences for eternal life–our present holiness.

Maybe holiness churches have tried so hard to keep up with generic "evangelicalism" for the sake of numerical growth that they have sacrificed their distinctive call to preach holiness "throughout the land." Indeed, in a culture of consumerism, preaching what people want to hear is easier than preaching the cost of discipleship. Unfortunately, evangelicalism often has a Calvinist slant. In this kind of milieu, the optimism inherent in the Wesleyan-Holiness message of Christian life is muffled. –Diane Leclerc, *Discovering Christian Holiness,* and Kevin DeYoung, *The Hole in Our Holiness*

2. HEADED IN THE WRONG DIRECTION!

This is a desperate time for America. It's difficult to be a follower of Jesus Christ. The nation is in trouble and moving in the wrong direction, clearly away from a predominantly Judeo–Christian point of view to a mostly postmodern, secular worldview. The transition has been both rapid and monumental in its ramifications. We have gone back to Judges 17:9, being a nation in which people have declared themselves in charge of their own lives and destiny. We have not committed ourselves to the purpose God has for each of us (vision), we are not willing to pay the price of becoming who God made and calls us to be (transformation), and we do not behave like Jesus because we do not think like him (worldview).

Trust in the institutions designed to foster appropriate living, from churches to the government, is plummeting. The political system has turned chaotic and unproductive. A majority of the country's churches seem to have lost sight of their God-given purpose and have proven to be ineffective in leading people back to the righteous path. Our responsibility is to understand God's vision for our lives, see the world through God's eyes and values, and then implement that vision as transformed, Christ-like servants of the eternal King. –George Barna, *America at the Crossroads*

3. EVERYTHING STARTS WITH GOD

The central concept among all Bible's teachings is God's holiness. God is "the Holy One" who is distinctly "other." God is marked off in nature from all that is ordinary, common, or human. God is unique, absolute perfection and purity. And yet, God also is holy Person, which means that the otherness does more than occasion a radical awe. It also brings a radical attractiveness that invites communion. The biblical God is the Father of Jesus Christ, uniquely separate and yet not remote and utterly removed. God's presence provokes awe while always seeking to relate, hoping to share his very life and holiness with us humans.

God has shown the divine holiness on our human level in Jesus Christ. The character of the life of Jesus is the manifestation of holiness in the flesh. Jesus "is the reflection of God's glory and the exact imprint of God's very being" (Heb. 1:3). Reports Paul: "Blessed be the God and Father of our Lord Jesus Christ, who has blessed us in Christ with every spiritual blessing in the heavenly places, just as he chose us in Christ before the foundation of the world to be holy and blameless before him in love" (Eph. 1:3-5). To be holy is to be blameless before God because of our acceptance of God's love for us in Christ. –James Earl Massey, *Views from the Mountain*

4. PENTECOST AS CENTRAL

Pentecost is the Jewish festival featured in the Book of Acts as the "birthday of the church." The Spirit of God came and life among the disciples of Jesus was greatly enriched. Gifts for ministry were given, as was the commission for worldwide mission. Recent generations of believers have rediscovered how crucial it is to be "pentecostal" in the sense of the Spirit of Jesus being central for the church's life. The New Testament speaks of the Spirit as teaching, gifting, leading, and commissioning the church. Jesus instructed his disciples not to go until the Spirit had come on them with power (Acts 1:8). Being transformed is prior to being deployed for service.

The Spirit is *God present*, not a doctrine or theory but a *living Person* active in our midst. The best of today's Christian theologians have begun thinking carefully about the Spirit as central for understanding the whole of the Christian gospel in our time. Note Jürgen Moltmann's *The Spirit of Life*, Clark Pinnock's *Flame of Love*, Ben Witherington's *The Shadow of the Almighty,* and Cheryl Bridges Johns' *Re-enchanting the Text*. In the book of Acts the Holy Spirit is seen as the divine agent and primary actor, causing some to call this key New Testament book the *Acts of the Holy Spirit*. The message for us? Wait, receive, and then go! When you do go, be agents of the Spirit in the way Steven Land subtitles his classic book, *Pentecostal Spirituality: A Passion for the Kingdom*. Holiness is God's "Godness." Being truly God's means that we will have on us a clear mark of that Godness.

5. CHRISTIAN PERFECTION

Does God expect people to become "perfect"? Jesus did say, "Be perfect, therefore, as your heavenly Father is perfect" (Matt. 5:48). This seems impossible, surely more a goal than an achievable state. Other Christians take it seriously as a present possibility, believing that God's grace is more powerful than the power of sin. The church is in definitional crisis and an expectancy drought about "sanctification." This statement may help. I will strive to open my life to the transforming power of God's perfecting love. God calls me to develop such a close and loving relationship with Jesus that I would never want to do anything to separate myself from that love or withhold it from anyone else. With that full intent, my 'sanctification' is real even if still in progress. That sounds very possible.

The church must develop practices designed to assist people in their spiritual disciplines. These are practical means crucial for receiving sanctifying grace. Congregations must be holiness training schools patterned after Christ who lived and died in perfect obedience to God. Believers in Jesus are to be "holy," that is, of the same mind and having the same love as Jesus. We are to press on, knowing that God is enabling us toward the fullness of Christ-likeness.

The One who began this good holiness work in us *will complete it* (Phil. 1:6). Forming us into the image of Jesus can be achieved in a moment so far as our decision is concerned. Completion of this divine work takes time and discipline, intentionality and a lifetime.
–Paul Chilcote, *Praying in the Wesleyan Spirit*, and Barry L. Callen, *All of God's Word for All of My Needs*

6. THE SPIRIT OF CHRIST ENABLES HOLINESS

Jesus is described as holy, his works holy, and through his Spirit he seeks to make God's people holy in attitude and action. The apostle Peter says this about Jesus and the people of God: "Come to him [Jesus], a living stone, though rejected by mortals yet chosen and precious in God's sight, and like living stones, let yourselves be built into a spiritual house to be a holy priesthood. You are a chosen race, a royal priesthood, a holy nation, God's own people" (1 Pet. 2:4-5, 9).

Once relieved of the guilt of past sin, believers are enabled to grow in holiness. It's the Holy One who chooses and calls his people to holiness. Holiness is based on the sacrifice of Jesus and conferred in the relationships of people with God. The Holy Spirit continues to work in and through the lives of believers, sanctifying them to love God with their whole heart, soul, mind, and strength, and to love their neighbors as themselves. The human response to Jesus' atonement involves faith and repentance. Christian life should come to involve willing obedience to the Holy Spirit who encourages believers to be, think, say, and act in accord with the very life of God.
–Kevin W. Mannoia and Don Thorsen, eds., *The Holiness Manifesto*

7. SELF-EMPTYING LOVE IS SANCTIFIED POWER

Jesus was very clear. In the kingdom of God, the last will be first; the poor, the mournful, the meek, and the hungry will be blessed and filled. The powerful in the world will be the least in the kingdom of God. Indeed, God's kingdom turns everything upside down. Authority is redefined. Mastery is minimized. Power is seen in paradox. In fact, the essence of God is self-emptying love. It's not in omnipotence but in God's choice toward *dis-ability* that Jesus reveals God best.

The cross-centered love of God known through Jesus is the same love to which we are called. It's a love perfected only in apparent weakness. Jesus' choice to humble himself, dis-able himself, calls us also to come and die, and to respect especially the disabled among us. Being "sanctified" does not make us whole in the sense of absolute perfection. Instead, it means that first we are perfectly loved. God looks with eyes of self-emptying love, and then we are to look at each other with the eyes of the same love. We pour ourselves out and are made whole (holy) together, not out of a position of power, but precisely because of our position of weakness, lived out in a self-emptying community of faith. –Don Thorsen and Barry L. Callen, *Heart & Life*

8. NO CHEAP DISCOUNT COUPONS

Are you ready to be transformed spiritually, exhaling the old life and inhaling the presence of God? Be warned. Being transformed by gaining the mind of Christ and growing into spiritual maturity is not a simple matter of instant gratification. It can't happen by using discount coupons passed out in church. It will take time, intentionality, and all you have. An old Cherokee was teaching his grandson about life. "A fight is going on inside us. It's between two wolves, one very good and one very evil." The boy said, "Which one will win?" The simple answer was, "The one you feed."

To be successful in growing toward Christ-likeness involves a careful feeding of the necessary process. Holiness is not about a lofty goal well beyond our reach. To be holy is not about *us* but about Jesus Christ *in us*. The goal is not to *be* him, of course, but to turn *toward* him and learn to reflect his image. We are not a people so much in need of new strategies for bringing people to Christ as we are people in need of truly seeking the face of God. It's God's radiant glory that will attract people, never to *us* but always to him. Holiness is living full of the Master who is holy. That creates wholeness in a way that integrates who we are inside with what we do in our behavior. God is the Master who is to become visible in and through us. –Kevin W. Mannoia, *Masterful Living*

9. EXHALING FOUL AIR

Genesis tells us that creation wasn't much until the breath of God swept over the waters. It was without form and densely dark but then took shape and blazed with light. We all need such formation and light, a re-creation of life that comes from God breathing graciously on us. It's time to exhale the foul air of our dark yesterdays and breathe in the wind of God's new creation. The Christian traditions, languages, and practices describe and enable this advance in varying ways. Progress in the life of faith is not automatic and rarely proceeds without some pain. Even so, there is great rejoicing in entering deeply into the mysteries of God.

Let's dare to join the journey to newness. Exhale the negative yesterdays and inhale the new-life breath of God. Dare to be "holy." What happened at Pentecost long ago provides the connecting link between past and present. The continuity between the historic presence of Jesus and our present salvation and call to ministry is disclosed in the living presence of the Spirit of Christ. The Kingdom of God announced and embodied by Jesus is not forced to wait on some future millennium. God came in Christ and still comes in the Spirit, for us and the world, and right now! –Barry L. Callen, *Catch Your Breath!*

10. THE EVERYWHERE PRESENCE OF GOD

God relates to all that exists by coming through the Spirit who is the everywhere presence of God. In Luke-Acts writing, the Holy Spirit is the agent at work from the time of Jesus' conception (Lk. 1:35) to the time of the church's ongoing witness to the resurrected Lord (Acts 2). The everywhere Spirit is God's way of being actively related to every person for the purpose either of bringing them to Christ or building them up into the fullness of Christ. This fulfills the Lord's promise, "You will receive power when the Holy Spirit has come upon you, and you will be my witnesses" (Acts 1:8).

The Holy Spirit is the everywhere presence of the redeeming God involved in our salvation from beginning to end. This is the Spirit of new birth continually renewing us. It's the Spirit providing a foretaste of the eternal newness awaiting us in the consummation.

Meanwhile, the fruit of the Spirit's presence provides and verifies godliness–love, joy, peace, patience, kindness, generosity, faithfulness, gentleness, and self-control. Paul refers to the Spirit's fruit as singular. To be truly of the Spirit means that all characteristics of the fruit are in evidence, for they are all of one piece. –Gilbert W. Stafford, *Theology for Disciples*

11. THE LUNG-FILLING WIND OF GOD

There are two clear ironies. Both are sad and suffocating. One is that "liberated" secular people today still find themselves bound by an emptiness that is deadening to their personal joy. The other is that many traditional Christians are also spiritually hungry and breathless despite their expressed faith and declared relationship with God in Christ. They may be believing all the right things but still have not breathed in the powerful, re-creating, lung-filling wind of God's gracious Spirit. To merely confess with the mouth is never enough. Things were different in the earliest years of the Christian church. The Holy Spirit was an *experience* more than a *doctrine*.

The church was a living fellowship, not yet a set of institutions with fixed leadership offices and detailed creeds. The mission life of the church began with the "not so fast!" instruction of Jesus. His disciples were to delay their urgent mission and first wait (Lk. 24:49). To be effective in life and mission, we believers are first to breathe in and taste the living Spirit of God. Only then are we prepared to share the good news of God through the Spirit with all people. E. Stanley Jones is a great example. He prayed: "O God, I need a Master. Chain me back into freedom. Darken me back into light. Stab me back into wholeness. Quiet me back into singing. Erase me back into fullness." –E. Stanley Jones, *Abundant Living*

12. IF CALVARY WERE THE END

C. S. Lewis' description of Narnia in *The Lion, the Witch, and the Wardrobe* is memorable. The wicked witch caused it to always be winter and never Christmas. What a hollow condition of despair. No hope. Empty suffering, much like it would be if there were no resurrection. Imagine the hopelessness if Calvary had been the end for

Jesus. His final destination, however, was not the cross or grave but the resurrection. He went through the cross and beyond the grave to get to us. Now he's asking us to go through a cross to get to our personal resurrection.

Even though Calvary always follows Gethsemane, be encouraged with the knowledge that, in Christ, after Calvary always comes the empty tomb (1 Cor. 15:20–22). At the empty tomb is resurrection to newness. Jesus was the "first fruits." We are intended to be the choice fruit that follows. What we do not have on the way to the tomb is detailed knowledge of how our lives will emerge into resurrection. Ours is the choice to surrender in faith, believing that the One to whom we surrender will work newness of life in us according to his will and in his own time and way. –Kevin W. Mannoia, *The Integrity Factor*

13. UNITY IN THE FURNACE OF CLEANSING

In every cold tomb life there lies waiting something about to burst forth! We must walk by faith, to be sure, but it's a holy walking guided by the Holy One and headed toward a holy goal. It requires placing all on the altar of refining fire--our God is a consuming fire. All efforts at Christian unity other than by a shared holiness are like pounding two pieces of cold, crooked iron against each other to make them fit together. The more blows the more distortions and differences. However, put them both into a furnace of white heat and soon they will lose their stiff and crooked individuality and flow into one mass. That is God's way of uniting his people in the common experience of the fire of the Holy Spirit's cleansing.

"Sanctification" is a set-apartness for God that leans in the direction of the reestablishment of right relationships with each other. The unity needed and possible among Christian believers comes through the dynamic of the Spirit's love. Love is the supreme gift given to the church. It's to supersede all forms of spiritual individualism and the exclusive dominance of particular church traditions. Union with God is not some "pantheism." We creatures always remain creatures, but ones caught up in relationship with the triune God. Being conformed to Christ, we share in the glory of God through fellowship with Father, Son, and Spirit (1 Jn. 1:3). –Barry L. Callen, *Christian Holiness*

14. FLYING AROUND A BARN

Jesus warned us not to build bigger barns, signs of greed and self-centeredness, but rather learn to fly around barns as a way of centering our lives on the fixed being of God. When learning to fly, I (Kevin) was instructed to practice doing "turns about a point." He was to select a fixed point on the ground, say a barn, and fly exact circles around it, compensating for the wind as he went. The nature and loving intentions of God are fixed realities on the ground of our lives. Christian holiness is learning to move through life by remaining fixed on and circling close to these eternal realities.

Stay fixed on God and other things tend to fix themselves. Is the center clear and immovable? Or is it relative and changing? Do we serve God or self and/or other people? All our activities should revolve around the divine center-point. If our flight paths are fixed, centered, there will be coherence, order, and effectiveness in our activities. If not, we'll soon be exhausted by trying to serve ourselves or other people who will move all over the landscape with expectations for us to keep circling them. Holiness is the proper fixedness, the controlled circling. –Kevin W. Mannoia, *The Integrity Factor*

15. A JOURNEY WITH CLEAR MARKERS

There lies before the Christian believer a lifetime of holy walking in the cleansing fires of God. God's power is perfected even in our weakness, although not necessarily all at once. We awaken to God as we walk with God over time. "As much as sin may abound, God's grace abounds even more" (Rom. 5:20). The holiness path to be walked has three key markers designated in two different ways biblically. The first is the *8–9–10* sequence found in 2 Corinthians 12:8–10. When trouble comes, we *reject, realize*, and *rejoice*. The second is in the Psalms. It's the *O-D-R* trail markers. When life goes wrong, the believer's experience should track from *orientation* to *disorientation* and finally to *re-orientation*. Jesus went this way himself, orientation (teachings and miracles) to disorientation (betrayal and brutal death) to re-orientation (dramatic resurrection).

These signs marking key stages along faith's path will humble and encourage us as we walk through the thorns and on to the glories. We learn along the way that the evil snake has its head cut off! We learn to live with comfort under the cloud of not knowing the answers to some of our perplexing questions about suffering and evil. God will show the way when there appears to be no way. We walk the holy way, proceeding in hope "that the creation itself will be set free one day from its bondage to decay and will obtain the freedom of the glory of the children of God" (Rom. 8:21). In the end, the holy end, resurrection trumps crucifixion! –Walter Brueggemann, *The Message of the Psalms*, and Barry L. Callen, *The Jagged Journey*

16. WHAT IT MEANS TO BE "SAVED"

Each of us is shadowed by a false self. Each false self wants to exist outside the reach of God's will and God's love, outside reality and life, on its own independent and disastrous course. Such a false and rebellious self is called sin. To say that I'm made in the image of God is to say that love is the reason for my existence, for God is love. *Selflessness* is my true self. Being without love cannot become love unless love, God, actively identifies me with himself. If God sends his own love, himself, to act in love in me and in all that I do, then I shall be transformed. I shall discover who I am and repossess my true identity by losing myself in the love of God.

To be "saved" is to be released from my immersion in the sea of lies and passions which is called "the world." I am released from the abyss of confusion and absurdity which is my own worldly self. The creative and mysterious inner self is delivered from the wasteful, hedonistic, and destructive ego that seeks only to cover itself with disguises. To be saved is to return to one's eternal reality and to live in the love of God. –Thomas Merton, *New Seeds of Contemplation*

17. PROXIMITY SHOULD BRING TRANSFORMATION

Proximity is the path to salvation. Salvation is the restoration of the image of God in us. We are not saved by doctrinal purity or propositional compliance. We are restored in the image of God when once again we are brought close to God in what may be called reconciliation. Being close to God, we regain and reflect the image God put within us from the beginning. Jesus is the singular path leading to that proximity and the dynamic force for its best accomplishment. He now has given the church the ministry of reconciliation, bringing back into close proximity what has become estranged and thus warped.

Even the church sometimes impedes the reconciliation it proudly preaches. We followers of Jesus construct within the church the same kind of walls that exist within society at large. We segregate ourselves by racial designations and allow our being male and female to separate us as God never intended. We exalt theological differences at the price of the intended unity and allow cultural diversity to be an excuse for awkward separations. We drain the strength of our divine mission, showing the world that apparently little has been changed by our claimed proximity to God. –Kevin W. Mannoia, "Proximity the Path to Transformation," *UniEvangelica*, and Curtiss Paul DeYoung, *Reconciliation*

18. SOUNDS IN THE SILENCE

In solitude, we can slowly unmask the illusion of our possessiveness and discover in the center of our own self that we are not what we can conquer, but what is given to us. In solitude, we can listen to the voice of him who spoke to us before we could speak a word, who healed us before we could make any gesture to help, who set us free long before we could free others, and who loved us long before we could show love to anyone.

It's in solitude that we discover that *being* is more important than *having*, and that we are worth more than the results of our best efforts. We discover that our life is not a position to be defended but a gift to be shared. We recognize that the love we can express is part of a greater love, and that the new life we bring forth is not property to cling to, but a gift to be received. –Henri J. Nouwen, *Out of Solitude*

19. PRAYER AS LIVING REALITY

Eugene Peterson is now famous for his masterful paraphrase of the Bible, *The Message*. If he's a modern master of communication, it didn't come easily. He grew up in a little Montana town hanging around the family butcher shop frequented by seedy characters. When Eugene became a Bible scholar, the sacred pages for him had to be more than some Elizabethan artifact. It had to be a living book appropriate for the gritty lives of butchers, cement-layers, and drunks. In the little Pentecostal church his family attended, "speaking in tongues" was a mark of the faithful. Eugene, a future linguist, wanted to be faithful but never could manage this special language. The inability plagued him.

When fifteen, a well-known Pentecostal teacher on "deep matters of the soul" stayed in the Peterson home and Eugene asked him privately, "How do you pray?" The answer shocked him. "I haven't prayed in forty years!" That startling statement eventually would become profound wisdom for Eugene. "Prayer wasn't something he did—it was something *he was*." Reports Eugene's biographer, "He was fascinated with language and crafting sentences." For him, Pentecostal prayer became how best to be a living prayer in part by stating the biblical text in language that goes beyond the mind to actually alter deep matters of the soul. –Winn Collier, *A Burning in My Bones*

20. STAND UP AND PRAISE GOD!

The more you praise God, the easier it is to stand. God is able to keep you from falling and present you faultless before the Father, so take time to worship. Draw near to God through praise. Be strengthened through praise. Be energized through praise. Be changed through praise. It's all right to raise your voice in praise. Sometimes what we are feeling is difficult to express in words. Express it in actions. I worry about people who never get excited about God. Something's wrong with their Christian experience.

Jesus gave a demonstration of his love for us, and every once in a while we ought to give him a demonstration of our love and devotion. We need to allow our emotions to be acted out. If God is in your heart, let it show on the outside. Available in the name of Jesus are forgiveness, healing, deliverance, power, whatever you need. Pursuing Jesus ignites the divine potential within for life's abundance. He gives exceeding great joy, eternal life now, and an activating of all the gifts and abilities he has placed in us to bring our God-given dreams to pass. Praise God! –Bishop Charles E. Blake, *Encountering God* and *Free to Dream*

Fill me with thy Spirit, Lord, fully save my longing soul;
Through the precious cleansing blood, purify and
make me whole . . . (Daniel S. Warner)

Come, Holy Spirit, I need you,
Come, sweet Spirit, I pray;
Come in your strength and your power,
Come in your own gentle way . . . (Gloria and William Gaither)

Thou hast cleansed me for Thy temple,
Garnished with Thy graces rare;
All my soul Thou art enriching,
by Thy fullness dwelling there . . . (Charles W. Naylor)

Thee we would be always blessing,
Serve Thee as Thy hosts above,
Pray and praise Thee, without ceasing,
Glory in Thy perfect love . . . (Charles Wesley)

The purest saint that lives below
does his own sanctity disclaim,
The wisest owns, I nothing know,
the holiest cries, I nothing am . . . (Charles Wesley)

Yes, this power from heaven descended,
with the sound of rushing wind;
Tongues of fire came down upon them,
as the Lord said he would send . . . (Charlie D. Tillman)

No more let sins and sorrows grow,
Nor thorns infect the ground.
He comes to make his blessings flow,
far as the curse is found . . . (Isaac Watts)

Thou whose purpose is to kindle,
Now ignite us with Thy fire;
While the earth awaits Thy burning,
with Thy passion us inspire . . . (David Elton Trueblood)

Since I met this blessed Savior,
since He cleansed and made me whole,
I will never cease to praise him,
I'll shout it while eternity rolls . . . (William J. Gaither)

Finish, then, Thy new creation,
pure and spotless let us be;
Let us see Thy great salvation,
perfectly restored in Thee . . . (Charles Wesley)

SOME NUGGETS ARE ESSENTIAL ROCKS

BUILD ONLY ON ROCK

Everyone who hears these words of mine and acts on them. Will be like a wise man who built his house on rock.
(Matt. 7:24-27)

The stone that the builders rejected has become the very head of the corner, and on it they often stumble and fall.
(1 Pet. 2:8)

The ones who scatter seeds on rock receive with joy but, because there are no roots, soon fall away.
(Lk. 8:13)

The Truths of God
For the People of God

Where two or three of you are gathered in my name, I am there among them. . . . And now I (Jesus) am no longer in the world, but they are in the world. Protect them in your name, Holy Father, so that they may be one as we are one.   (Matt. 18:20; Jn. 17:11)

You are fellow citizens with the saints, and members of the household of God, built on the foundation of the apostles and prophets, with Christ Jesus himself as the cornerstone. . . . As in one body, we have many members and not all members have the same function, so we who are many are one body in Christ. (Eph. 2:19-20; Rom. 12:4-6)

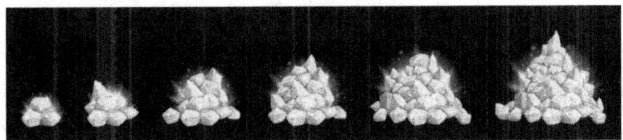

VI

The Community that Faithfully Serves

Is the crowd you know at church obviously the Bride of Christ, clearly the divine beachhead actively transforming this world by being the spearhead of God's arriving kingdom? How do you react to this negative assessment? "Americanization has turned many Christian congregations into marketplaces for religious consumers, ecclesiastical businesses energized by impressive motivational rhetoric" (Eugene H. Peterson). If true, is that the church *of Jesus* or of someone else?

The following twenty-four golden nuggets of Christian truth attempt to highlight a range of characteristics that should make our churches all that Jesus intends for his chosen bride. May our commitments and the Spirit of Jesus working among us make it so! Oh, to be the church that God actually intends and is anxious to enable. It's to be filled with folks who are in awe of the loving God, full of respect for the revealed Word, and increasingly putting on Christ as they mature and serve together as instruments of the Spirit.

Glimpses of the following Golden Nuggets

1. There are many movies about "aliens." What of the church?
2. The Bible is not a religious encyclopedia.
3. Since God is a united community, we had better be one too.
4. Is the church really the church when it's asleep.
5. Do you know the church's reformist heritage of the church?
6. We need to get straight the real meaning of "radical."

7. The church must be committed to each "ortho."
8. Cross-work is the courageous calling of the church.
9. What is the church to be doing to avoid anxiety and despair?
10. "Backsliding" is playing religion while on our backs.
11. What about the the families of foreigners?
12. Can you smell the terrible "Rs" of traditionalism.
13. Tomorrow is already here, so start ministering.
14. Picket fences walls allow better working and serving.
15. Church unity is essential and impossible, at least for us.
16. Dynamite the dirt on your own doorstep!
17. It's God's church, and God is on the move! Are you?
18. Could the church begin holding meetings that really meet?
19. The "love feast" is an excellent way to really meet.
20. There are three compelling elements to be present.
21. You aren't your own and the church isn't yours.
22. Stop the endless, crowd-pleasing religious babbling!
23. The practical and the academic are a but necessary pair.
24. Church mission is stewardship of the whole world.

1. DARE TO BE A RESIDENT ALIEN!

We awoke a few years ago and realized that almost nobody believed it today. We now meet few young parents, college students, or auto mechanics who believe that one becomes Christian by simply breathing the air and drinking the water in the hospitable environment of Christendom America. For our parents, the church was the only show in town. Church, home, and state joined to form a national consortium that worked together to at least instill "Christian values." Now things are different. Only when the church dares to enact the scandalous, Jesus-centered tradition will it truly be the body of Christ that can survive with integrity and even transform such a new world.

The church of Jesus must regain its vitality and capacity to nourish souls in the face of the illusions, pretentions, and eroding values of today's new and quite secular world. The church is to be a colony, an island of one culture in the middle of another very different. In baptism, our citizenship is transferred from one dominion to another and we become *resident aliens*.

To be resident but alien is a formula for loneliness that few of us can sustain. Believers are to be corporate beings. After telling the Philippian church to "have this mind among yourselves which is yours in Christ Jesus," Paul also tells them, "God is working in you both to will and work for his good pleasure." He then reminds them of who they are–or must become. "Our Commonwealth is in heaven" (3:20). –Stanley Hauerwas and William H. Willimon, *Resident Aliens*

2. THE SPIRIT, BIBLE, CHURCH

The mission of God's Spirit is to complete the program of the Triune God in this world. The Spirit is the agent bringing into being the new creation to (2 Cor. 5:17). To this end, the Spirit inspires and speaks through the Bible and thus bears witness to Jesus Christ and gives direction and power for the mission of the church. The Spirit's inspiration originally brought the Bible into existence, ensuring that the written result adequately reflects the intent of God. The Spirit continues to illumine the holy text, helping people understand the truth and intent of these collected documents. The Spirit illumines our minds and makes the Bible "come alive," causing the people of God to understand its significance for their life together in the present time.

Early church leaders experienced the power and truth of the Spirit of God through the biblical writings, knowing them as "animated with the Spirit of Christ." The Bible, then, is the deposit of divine revelation, human words that in some marvelous way also function as the Word of God. The Bible is foundational for the church in every generation because it provides the interpretive framework for the Christian mission. It orients our present on the basis of the past and in accord with a divine vision for the future as the Spirit provides. –Stanley J. Grenz, *Theology for the Community of God*

3. EVEN GOD IS A COMMUNITY

Becoming a member of the community of faith, the church, is not an optional matter for the Christian believer. It's critical to the very nature of God and humanity. The doctrine of the "Trinity" forms the heart of the Christian conception of God. It suggests that God is himself *relational*. The Father, Son, and Spirit comprise the social Trinity. Therefore, community is not merely an aspect of human life. It lies within the very divine essence. God is relational within the divine being and reaches relationally in love to be in community with those created to also be in community.

What then is the church? It's the special people who know themselves to be standing together in relationship to the God who saves them. It's the fellowship in which disciples teach and support each other. It's the holy assembly of those who live and serve in righteousness by the grace of God and through the presence and power of God's Spirit. Since God is a community of actively relating love, his people are to be exactly that, the people called together to reflect the loving and reaching divine image to the world. –Stanley J. Grenz, *Theology for the Community of God*

4. THE SLUMBER OF DISTRACTION

The evangelical Christian movement of the 20th century has tended to blunt the tendency toward social engagement that should come naturally to holiness people. Within the American church context, and in contrast to the church's 19th-century advocacy for the abolition of slavery, the elevation of women's rights, and needed economic reforms, the holiness movement was generally sidelined during the civil rights movement of the 1950s and 1960s. The very people who should have been pressing the principles of Christian faith into culture were themselves silent behind firewalls of defensiveness. They feared others assuming that cultural engagement was a theological liberalism or spiritual capitulation.

As we now emerge from this slumber of distraction, and in some cases just indifference, we must shake off the obsession with eliminating differences among ourselves. Sameness is not our Christian goal. Expanding the Kingdom of God is. This does not mean that we should give up healthy discourse about the worth of "orthodoxy." It does mean that we upbuild one another and always remember our real mission, tempering our individual extremes. –Kevin W. Mannoia, "A Case for Engagement" and "The Diversity of Unity" (with T. D. Jakes).

5. DISCOVERING THE REAL HERITAGE

Torn between evangelicalism and the imperatives of the civil rights movement, I chose the latter with a bad conscience acquired through years of conditioning in the evangelical world. I then took up the study of the roots of my denomination, the Wesleyan Church, and discovered to my surprise that the denomination was a product of a close parallel to the civil rights movement, the abolitionist protest against slavery in the period just before the Civil War. A perfectionist aspiration had flourished between 1840 and 1865 and was the driveshaft of social reform. I hadn't known that!

The founders of my denomination were advocates of principles to which I had come to believe deeply. I discovered that my denomination was not unique but shared a reformist heritage with other aspects of evangelicalism. I had been struggling with the wrong end of evangelical currents that once had reverberated with vitality and reform activity but had over the course of a century fallen into a form of decadence. I had discovered the real heritage, the one I actively affirm. The church is not to be sitting on the sidelines. –Donald W. Dayton, *Discovering an Evangelical Heritage,* and Timothy L. Smith, *Revivalism and Social Reform*

6. A RADICAL COMMUMITY

The dynamic ideal of the experience of Christian perfection functioned within early Methodism to sustain hope and optimism in the present spiritual life. It served as a spur toward discipline and a high moral and ethical quest. A basic intent of the church of Jesus Christ is the distinctive witness of the Christian community, the church, a body very different from the world. John Wesley was a "radical" Christian because he understood that Christianity is not so much a system of doctrine as it is the experience of the body of Christ in community as matured and active discipleship.

The effective struggle for social justice begins with building a biblically faithful community of justice-seeking Christian disciples. What the world needs now is "radical" Christianity. In 2000 years the church has not noticeably improved on the gospel or the biblical picture of Christian community and discipleship. The church has always been most faithful when having gone back to its biblical roots. Then it's free to be most creative in challenging the spiritual, social, and economic crises of its day. Going back to the original basics is to be "radical" in the proper way. –Howard A. Snyder, *The Radical Wesley*

7. FELLOWSHIP IS MORE THAN RIGHT BELIEF

John Wesley properly qualified his description of the church. He emphasized that the church ought to be more than a congregation of "faithful persons." It also should be exhibiting "living faith." It's to be more than a community of right belief (*orthodoxy*), but also one of right heart (*orthokardia*) and right practice (*orthopraxis*). Someone can hold correct opinions and be a stranger to "religion of the heart." The church should be constituted by true believers who are committed deeply to all three "orthos."

What unifies the true church? It's hardly agreement on every doctrine and theological issue. That would require removing every Christian outside one's particular understanding of the church and its teachings and practices. Certainly we can't be indifferent to teachings or practices clearly contrary to the Bible and historic Christianity. However, not everyone interprets the Bible the same way. Nor has every development in doctrine, worship, and congregational life in church history been understood the same way. Flexibility rather than rigidity is needed in the fellowship of Christians and their churches. –Don Thorsen, *Calvin vs Wesley*

8. NO ONE AN ISLAND

Martin Luther King, Jr., had a heart that beat with much the same rhythm as John Wesley's. King's close Wesleyan-Holiness friend, James Earl Massey, explains. The leading theme among King's many public presentations was his great concern for *community*. He tried to help us understand the nature of community, the need for community, and the concern of God that we be open to experiencing community. He was forever reminding us about the importance of *persons* and the effects on them of relationships they were experiencing. The nation and church can find themselves only as people live *communally*.

Dr. Massey also preached reconciliation into true community. He called the church to *Cross-work*. For each of us there is a vertical dimension in our experience as Christians. We are reconciled individually by God through Christ. Then there is a horizontal dimension since we are to interact creatively with fellow believers. The vertical and horizontal together form a cross. Our sacrificial task as reconcilers is inspired by love, courageously faces divisive walls of hostility and hate, and learn to do this together with courageous cross-work. –James Earl Massey, *Views from the Mountain*

9. FREEING THE CHURCH OF ANXIETY

The Western church presently is immersed in yet another age of anxiety. Like previous such ages, the present is characterized by pessimism and despair over the current state of the church and uncertainty about its future. The core problem is how to discern the presence, power, and speaking of the Spirit to the church. It was that divine voice that originated the church and can renew it in our time. The Spirit is still speaking of the same Lord. "As for the mystery of the seven stars that you saw in my right hand and the seven golden lampstands: the seven stars are the angels of the seven churches, and the seven lampstands are the seven churches" (Rev. 1:20).

And the Spirit's message to these churches? Here are the things the churches are to be hearing and supposed to be doing when in that original womb of Pentecost. They were supposed to be waiting on the Lord in prayer, focusing on the reception and celebration of the Holy Spirit, humbly repenting and being baptized, studying doctrine, praising the Holy Trinity in a spirit of thanksgiving, and having deep concern for one another's welfare and a vital witness to Jesus Christ. Doing these in any day helps the church discern the current voice of the Spirit and thus dispense with a disabling anxiety. –Jason Vickers, *Minding the Good Ground*

10. LET'S LIMIT THE "REVIVALS"

When I was young, the Christian congregations I knew held two week-long "revivals" each year. I always wondered why believers kept dying and needing to be revived every six months. The hope, of course, was to reach new believers as well as to salvage old ones, but I watched the old ones dominating attendance and regularly seeking spiritual new life. "Backsliding" was a common word. It was the tendency of the already renewed to fall backwards into sin. We should hear Paul well. "You groped your way through that murk once, but no longer. You're out in the open now. The bright light of Christ makes your way plain. So no more stumbling around. Get on with it!" (Eph. 5:8-9).

There's a long history of God's people being unfaithful. They go through good-looking religious motions and yet become satisfied being "religious" while being crooked in their hearts and actions. We disciples should never look for loopholes or dare to take shortcuts in receiving, being changed by, and sharing God's truth and love. Of little use are human designs and religious platitudes and routines. They risk the finished product having our human names over the church door. When that happens, regardless of well-publicized headlines about great things happening inside, God wouldn't be there. It would be time for another revival! –Barry L. Callen, with Steve Hoskins, *A Year with Rabbi Jesus* and *God in the Shadows*

11. COMPASSION AND SOCIAL ADVOCACY

Christians have long been recognized for acts of compassion for those who suffer from poverty, illness, and homelessness. We have ministered sacrificially against the *symptoms* of impoverishment. But what about their *causes*? This requires advocacy on behalf of collective, societal, and political causes that lead to the unjust treatment of people, often because of their racial ethnicity, gender, age, ability, language, nationality, sexual orientation, or religious backgrounds. Should Christians be concerned about such so-called "social" injustices?

God's people in the Bible certainly were! In Acts 6 we learn that complaints arose among members of the early church because Hellenist widows were being neglected in the distribution of food. These widows were from a minority ethnic and possibly racial group and may have had different linguistic, cultural, and possibly national backgrounds. The disciples of Jesus responded immediately to this injustice by establishing deacons—a role within the church dedicated to serving those outside as well as inside one's own community. This is one of many biblical examples of believers responding to social injustice. Failing to do so is hardly being the church. –Don Thorsen, *What's True about Christianity?*

12. MY SKIN JUST CRAWLS

A mature churchman announced late in life that a square of chocolate doesn't produce welts on his skin nor does the mere sight of goldenrod send him into a fit of sneezing. But he had developed other allergies. He's now allergic to those who fly high on Sunday but can't walk straight on Monday or don't pay their bills on Tuesday. He's very allergic to chronic complainers who project their own inadequacies on leaders of the church. He has trouble with calamity howlers who equate their own defeat of spirit with decline in the spiritual life and power of the church.

Another wise churchman identified the terrible "Rs" of traditionalism in church life. *Rote* is routinely repeating doctrines and practices of the faith until their meaning is gone. Rote leads to *Rut*, getting stuck in a ditch of one's own making and insisting that others comply or are just wrong. Rote and Rut end in *Rot*. When water stops flowing it stagnates. Christians quite satisfied with their spiritual growth and thinking soon develop the smell of deterioration that disturbs the nostrils of God. A friend used to say, "when you're green you grow, when ripe you rot." –Barry L. Callen, *The Wisdom of the Saints*

13. TOMORROW IS HERE TODAY!

The church should be nothing short of the fellowship of *tomorrow's* people who are sharing with Christ the urgent task of rearranging the realities of *today's* world by the power of the Spirit of all time. Then, someday, with time behind us, eternity before us, and the redeemed of all ages around us, there will be heaven, our final and forever home. In the meantime, we must refuse to be paralyzed by the idea of an eventual paradise. Our churches must be about God's business *now*.

God's future isn't waiting for a distant reality to arrive. Jesus once made this dramatic announcement: "Times up! God's kingdom *is here*. Change your life" (Mark 1:15, The Message). No one is ready to really live *here and now* until matters of the *there and then* are faced. The fruits of then are to be emerging and being applied now. We sinful humans tend to be dead until death is faced and real future life begins to dominate our present moments. –Barry L. Callen, *Caught Between Truths* and *The Living Dead*

14. RESHAPING TODAY'S CHURCH

The Church of Jesus has a dynamic nature. It's not static, not changeless. There is freshness in the ongoing work of God intended to shape the church in each time and place. The church is to be a dynamic movement of the Spirit, a spiritual revolution, always apostolic in nature and present in orientation. Embracing this dynamic movement is necessary to be a true partner with the Holy Spirit in forming the body of Christ. The church of tomorrow is finding true unity in the center and not in drawing perimeters and being exclusive. Embracing diversity is a first step to unity.

Church traditions can lead to traditionalism which drains vitality and relevance. Block walls that divide must give way to picket fences that define our differing heritages while still allowing us to reach through to each other in collaboration and common mission. Walls may keep someone else's weeds from our backyard but they also keep the flowers of others from gracing ours. In the future, the fences defining Christian groups must be more relational and descriptive and less prescriptive and divisive. –Kevin W. Mannoia, *Church 2 K*

15. A HEALTHY AND UNIFIED FAITH COMMUNITY

The most mature disciples of Jesus know their limitations and their need for the wisdom and fellowship of the whole body of Christ, past and present, the traditional and contemporary, the Eastern and the Western, some called "Evangelical" and others "Pentecostal" or "Catholic." All are regularly present in the body's life, and each needs to be open to the guidance and gifting of the Spirit, the whole body's primary resource and guide. Unity in the Body of Christ is essential for effective outreach. Pluralism is becoming the global norm, as unfortunately is the tendency toward defensiveness and the quest for dominance.

There are so many lines of difference. Unity seems insurmountable, and that's the joy of it. Unity in the church is impossible, *for us*. But God is not ordered according to our patterns or contained by our structures or limited to our possibilities. In Him there is energy that surpasses our ability. In that we should take hope. Only God can bring the unity for which Jesus prayed (Jn. 17). --Kevin W. Mannoia, "Pluralism Is Here" and "Kingdom Chaos: The Joy of Finding Unity"

16. WHAT POWER IS ADEQUATE TO TRANSFORM?

Jesus was teaching confidence in the supremacy and endurance of God's kingdom over all human institutions, philosophies, governments, and empires. Such confidence makes secondary all group nationalisms. It settles the citizenship question. We are to give Caesar only what belongs to him (Matt. 22:21), and that's less than he likely will demand. Our prayer to the Father should be, "*Yours* is the kingdom and the power!" The Holy Spirit provides the *dunamis* (Greek for "dynamite") of God that transforms life and makes Christian life and ministry possible. "Stay here in the city until you have been clothed with power from on high" (Lk. 24:49).

No church can succeed when full of spiritually powerless grumblers. Folks sometimes come to church and go away finding fault. One usually sees what's being looked for and expected. The solution? Come with an eye focused on the glory of God. Come to get good and do good. Look for the virtues and good qualities in brothers and sisters in the faith. Apply the sermon to your own life and let the other person alone. Keep your own doorstep well swept and you'll be too busy to focus on the presumed dirt on the doorsteps of others. –Barry L. Callen, *The Prayer of Holiness-Hungry People* and *The Wisdom of the Saints*

17. TWO TEMPTATIONS TO AVOID

Two serious temptations face the contemporary church. Some Christian bodies become more concerned about maintaining their separate movements *within* the church than about aligning themselves with the far larger Jesus movement. That's sectarianism. The temptation of others is to try to replicate a New Testament structural church pattern perceived to be singularly approved by God. Such replication is impossible. There is the unrelenting pressure of contemporary circumstances and the collective historical experience of the church that inevitably influence whatever we do. We can't fully extract ourselves from who we are at a given time.

Legitimate movements within the church are part and parcel of its historic life. The church established by Jesus is a divine movement. Movements within the church often serve the Spirit's purposes and then cease to exist, but the Jesus movement itself is destined to continue to the end of time. Final loyalty must not lie with who *we* are or how *we* have things set up at the moment. When the missionary impulse is lacking, it usually indicates that a movement in church life is stagnating. It's God's church, and God always is on the move! –Gilbert W. Stafford, *Theology for Disciples*

18. MEETINGS THAT REALLY MEET

Martin Buber wrote, "all real living *is meeting*." We all need personal relationships filled with understanding and depth. Unfortunately, our culture encourages work, study, and even worship without our coming to know each other as real persons. The New Testament Gospels are full of stories about Jesus really meeting people. Zacchaeus met Jesus and his life was changed. Can we learn to risk giving ourselves to each other in real meetings that are life-changing? Jesus promised to be present "where two or three come together [seriously not incidentally] in my name" (Matt. 18:20).

The church may be thought of as an ongoing *corporate conversation*, believers continuing to explore together who they are and are to be as a body on mission for Christ. Such conversation requires very intentional togetherness and the skill of listening, not just talking. Each learns from the others if all are really paying attention. Real life in Christ is really meeting each other as the Spirit is meeting and ministering to each. –D. Michael Henderson, *John Wesley's Class Meeting: A Model for Making Disciples*

19. STAGING FEASTS OF LOVE

An assumption of the early Wesleyan movement deserves careful attention by Christian churches of all times and affiliations. It was the regularly planned gathering of believers around a common vision of the Christian life, a gathering designed for significant help in the spiritual maturation of all involved. John Wesley had concluded that any model of spiritual growth that relied exclusively on the individual pursuit of holiness was unwise and quite inadequate. "The gospel of Christ knows no religion but social, no holiness but social holiness." It cannot flourish without society, without living and actively conversing with others.

Some hymn words sung were: "Help us to help each other, Lord, each other's cross to bear; let each his friendly aid afford, and feel his brother's care." Wesley adapted an earlier expression of communal support called the "love feast," considering it a continuation of the early Christian *agape meal*. He elevated the role of testimonies by believers. The hope was that these shared stories of spiritual challenges and progress would model and encourage the entire group along the way of salvation. They were to be a highly personal means through which God works in the love feast to "nourish us with social grace." –Randy L. Maddox, *Responsible Grace*

20. EMBRACE DIVERSITY, STICK TO THE CENTER

The increasing diversity of the church in our world today invites the maturing Christian to embrace such diversity as a first step to unity. Rather than drawing a perimeter and staying exclusive, the truth of tomorrow requires finding true unity in the center, Jesus Christ. We then can embrace better the diversity of God's kingdom among us. With so much time, energy, and emphasis given to methods of church life and mission, we have almost forgotten the deeper message, the centerpiece of our mission.

If we could put serious time into discussing our mission and the power that unity in our diversity brings to that mission, perhaps we wouldn't be wringing our hands at the decline of so many churches. The three most compelling elements of the church ahead of us are church mission, unity, and leadership. Center on these and see how the rhetoric, activities, and passions of emerging leaders will flow together. –Kevin W. Mannoia, *Church 2K*

21. THE SPIRIT'S PASSION—EVANGELISM

Understanding church mission is perhaps the best path to Christian unity. Churches have a prophetic vocation in the world, a calling to be agents of transformation within the wider community of humanity. This is to be pursued without the church becoming one with the world. It's to be *in* the world without being *of* the world (Jn. 17:11, 16; 1 Jn. 2:15-17). Aspects of this mission include proclaiming the gospel of Christ in word and deed, caring for those suffering and in need, and advocating on behalf of the poor and marginalized. Evangelism represents an important part of the church's mission, but not all of it.

The Bible speaks about sharing the gospel in both deed and word (Eph. 4:11). Evangelism is to be not a program but a passion, a heavenly constraining of the soul. Rabbi Jesus said that his disciples are to go into all the world, but first to stay put. Don't attempt to engage in the assigned mission until equipped with power from on high. We will never make it on our own, but we need never be alone on the frontlines of kingdom work. We are to go only after we are filled and infused and empowered by God's Spirit. Without the Spirit, only frustration and failure follow. Kingdom work requires kingdom gifts, and the Spirit is the essential Gift and gift giver in the kingdom of God. –Barry L. Callen, with Steve Hoskins, *A Year with Rabbi Jesus*

22. PRAYERS THAT TRANSCEND TIME AND PLACE

The people of God have no higher calling than to be a house of prayer (1 Kings 8:22–53; Isa. 56:7). Jesus urged his disciples to avoid further burdening the Father's tired ears with more fancy, endless, calculated, crowd-pleasing religious babbling. We cannot earn divine attention by emotion, verbosity, or intriguing logic. The disciple's prayers are to be childlike, not childish but humble, the kind that would stick in the throats of the proud. Our prayers are to be couched in reverence, admit to ignorance, and ask only for the glory of God, necessary bread, and needed forgiveness and redemption.

The church's prayers should not be delivered alone. We should commune with all the saints. There must be strong connections maintained in the church, some transcending time and space. Current Christians must recall with profit the faithfulness of earlier generations of believers. Only then can the faithful of today be at their best in passing on the faith to each other and eventually to many yet unborn. There's so much to be learned from yesterday, whatever its limitations. Our forebears have run the whole race of faith and now are waiting with valuable stories to share. May we be time-transcending, big-picture, corporate followers of Jesus. –Barry L. Callen, *with Steve Hoskins, A Year with Rabbi Jesus* and *The Prayer of Holiness-Hungry People*

23. NEEDED: THE PRACTICAL AND THE ACADEMIC

The recent energetic activity of local churches in reaching their communities has outstripped seminaries in their ability to prepare new leaders to meet these missional needs. As aggressive and entrepreneurial church leaders experiment in highly pragmatic ways, the academy has been found wanting. The rapidity of shifting leadership paradigms and the unique phenomenon of proliferating mega churches has left theological educators at the drafting table designing strategies of response that are quickly obsolete. In the current microwave culture of the North American evangelical church, value is placed on sound-byte education, highly specialized skills, and immediate practical results.

This preference for the instantaneous will doubtless change. Meanwhile, seminaries are compelled to fulfill their mission to educate persons in accordance with the expectations of the academy and its accrediting bodies. Both such expectations and the practical needs of the churches are noble and necessary. One without the other brings serious deficiencies in church life. Together they demand exceptional flexibility and wisdom. –Kevin W. Mannoia, in *In Trust* magazine

24. WE ARE STEWARDS OF ALL CREATION

God himself is whole, and what God creates reflects such integration and wholeness. Our human condition seeks to compartmentalize and thereby skew our vision of creation and church mission.

With a siloed approach to Christian responsibility, there is a tendency toward greater emphasis on the spiritual and eternal, while overshadowing and minimizing the importance of the immediately observable, physical, and certainly ecological.

A strategy of the enemy of our faith is to confound the work of God in the world by narrowing our focus and encouraging a short-sighted mission myopia. Our vision of a new creation should invite a holistic, integrated engagement with all dimensions of our existence, including our surroundings and how we treat and use them. What God created we are to steward responsibility. God's creation is not another commodity to be consumed as we wish. Our privilege is to manage all things as God's possessions as we travel our salvation journey toward "all things becoming new." –Kevin W. Mannoia, in *Christian Ecology & Stewardship*

> We are God's people, the chosen of the Lord,
> born of his Spirit, established by his Word . . .
> (Bryan Jeffery Leech)
>
> He bids us build each other up,
> and gathered into one,
> to our high calling's glorious hope,
> we hand-in-hand go on . . . (Charles Wesley)
>
> There's a love we feel in Jesus,
> there's a manna that he feeds us,
> It's a promise that he gives us
> when we gather in his name . . . (Tedd Smith)
>
> I love Thy kingdom, Lord,
> the home of Thine abode;
> the church our blessed Redeemer saved
> with his own precious blood . . . (Timothy Dwight)

Elect from every nation,
yet one o'er all the earth,
Her charter of salvation,
one Lord, one faith, one birth . . . (Samuel J. Stone)

The church of Christ in every age,
beset by change, but Spirit lead,
must claim and test its heritage
and keep on rising from the dead . . . (Fred Pratt Green)

God over all and in us all,
through sister and through brother,
no power on earth or hell withal
Can rend us from each other . . . (Daniel S. Warner)

Blest be the tie that binds
our hearts in Christian love;
The fellowship of kindred minds
is like to that above . . . (John Fawcett)

In Christ, there is no East or West,
in him no South or North,
but one great fellowship of love
throughout the whole wide earth . . . (Jonathan Oxenham)

SOME NUGGETS ARE ESSENTIAL ROCKS

ROCKS PRODUCE AND SEDUCE

The Lord said to Moses, "Go ahead of the people. I will be standing there in front of you on the rock at Horeb. Strike it and water will come out of it so that the people may drink."
(Ex. 17:6)

You shall not make for yourselves idols or erect any carved images or pillars, and you shall not place figured stones in your land to worship them, for I am the Lord, your God.
(Lev. 26 :1-4)

They sacrificed to demons, not to God. "You were unmindful of the Rock that bore you. You forgot the God who gave you birth."
(Deut. 32:17-18)

The Truths of God
For the People of God

May you be made strong with all the strength that comes from God's glorious power, so that you may have all endurance and patience, giving thanks to the Father, who has enabled you to share in the inheritance of the saints in the light. (Col. 1:11-12).

God's foolishness is wiser than human wisdom, and God's weakness is stronger than human strength. . . . Finally, be strong in the Lord, and in his mighty power. (1 Cor. 1: 25; Eph. 6:10)

VII

The Life that Boldly Empowers

Life is a journey. The life of Christian faith can be both a treacherous voyage and an exhilarating ride! It's goal is not judged by the score of our "achievements" since we're not "earning" anything by "good works." It's a faith journey launched and guided and judged by divine grace. Since it's about God, for God's purposes, and moving toward destiny with God, the Christian life is possible only because God lovingly makes it so, calling, coming, enlivening, directing, and empowering. True life in Christ is existence for the mission of the Spirit of Jesus who gifts, accompanies, and comforts.

Following are twenty-six golden nuggets of Christian truth and testimony that enable and propel the Christian spiritual life. Don't travel without them! Their intent is like that of A. B. Simpson and other holiness reformers of the nineteenth century. The intent is resuscitation of the believed dead or at least the awakening of an anemic church. Those having already experienced "conversion" need to move on to "full salvation," to their "full inheritance." This deeper experience is not just for a pious few but the will of God for all believers. The fellowship of Jesus lacking members with this fullness and depth will hardly be able to function well as the church of Jesus.
–Bernie A. Van De Walle, *The Heart of the Gospel*

Glimpses of the following Golden Nuggets

1. Our Abba is our spiritual action dynamic.
2. Dare to shine in darkness where the evil one waits.
3. Minimalists are saved from the past but not yet holy.
4. There must be bonds of fellowship that transcend pride.
5. Being "fools" for Christ is the eccentricity of Christians.
6. Following Christ is surely not for the fainthearted.
7. Forget the periods and stick with the commas—it's not over!
8. The Kingdom is the great equalizer. Focus on the center.
9. Doubt can expose false securities and idolatrous views.
10. There is no set formula, only the power of divine grace.
11. Let justice roll down like life-giving waves of water.
12. Standard human language can break down.
13. The singing of the Psalms and the hope of Isaiah.
14. Fulfilling the Law is always practicing the Law of Love.
15. Don't remember so that you can find ways to get even.
16. Performance-based identity is the top of the iceberg.
17. Some signs and sins are to be noted carefully.
18. "Eternal" life is reflecting God's own life.
19. Religion may be escapist, but not always!
20. We've got to do God's business God's way.
21. The merits of Christ's atonement can reach all people.
22. Are human governments to be obeyed or resisted? Yes.
23. What are safeguards against sin?
24. We need the fathers and mothers to for the fuller picture.
25. Do you have a life testimony like this special man?
26. Always keep a bungee cord in your suitcase.

1. CHRISTIAN SPIRITUALITY

Christian spirituality has to do with our relationship with the divine Spirit--with God who in Scripture is revealed as the presence of our heavenly Father, our *Abba*. This is a term of personal intimacy. God is known in Jesus Christ and people are reconciled to God through him by grace through faith. Jesus promised that the Holy Spirit would continue to work in and through the lives of believers, healing, restoring, and transforming them spiritually. God's Spirit works with sanctifying and commissioning grace.

"Salvation" is as much for this life as for life hereafter. In Scripture as well as church history, many activities, exercises, and disciplines of spiritual importance have been practiced. God graciously intends for them to serve as means by which believers may grow in faith, hope, and love, in intimacy of their personal relationship with God, and in obedient maturation into Christlikeness that impacts this world for good. –Don Thorsen, *Pocket Dictionary of Christian Spirituality*

2. WHERE THE DEVIL WAITS

Karl Marx was just wrong. Christianity, at least when lived as it should be, is not a mere opiate that helps people cope with the real world. When Jesus was breathing his last, he was speaking words of forgiveness. When heading toward the cross, he did anything but run away from trouble. Suffering had to be faced and a world redeemed. We present disciples of Jesus have to learn that true faith shines forth especially when it hurts. Jesus had to face temptations in the desert. He knew the Devil was waiting. The Lord proceeded to soil his reputation among the religious leaders by hanging out in the haunts of lost, lonely, and searching people who weren't religiously respectable.

Being the Lord's disciples today carries no guarantee of constant comfort, safety, and even respectability in the eyes of some. All real disciples must be willing to serve in the shadows and absorb some undeserved pain. We must not ingest spiritual opiates but be daring salt for the earth. Jesus tends to be found where hurting humanity huddles. To be true light in this darkened world, a disciple must

be willing to shine from inside the darkness, right where the devil waits. It's been said that the world will be destroyed not by those doing evil but by those watching them and doing nothing about it.
–Barry L. Callen, *Catch Your Breath!* and *God in the Shadows*

3. LOWLY PATHS OF FULL SALVATION

The paradox of the way of full salvation is that the higher path is a lowly path that challenges us with the toughest choices. Such lowly paths require us to make sacrifices for social good and not personal gain. The higher but lowly paths require the courage to let go of the lesser ambitions of self-advancement for the greater ambitions of God's kingdom of grace, generosity, and compassion. They invite us to become big enough to choose smallness, whatever our place in the social strata. That's where we will find the treasure, the meaning of our humanity, the real fullness of life.

Unfortunately, a great many people identify as Christians but are only culturally or institutionally so. Many are in a static state of beginning salvation. They have come to a stop. There is no progress forward from the starting gate. Their spiritual odometer shows little mileage and their spiritual formation is stunted. They are minimalists, saved from past sin but not aspiring to holiness. They haven't traveled very far down the lowly paths of true Kingdom life. –Jonathan S. Raymond, *Social Holiness*

4. GOOD NEWS TO ALL PEOPLE

The consequence of John Wesley's thought and ministry is a worthy example for all believers. He makes the graces of holy love accessible to all people, especially the poor, the very least of all. Invited to participate in one of his "class meetings," the downtrodden came to know themselves as mistakenly labeled lazy and shiftless. Instead, they were people being invited to receive the richest love and the most profound graces. The destitute no longer were being alienated but embraced and empowered, no longer forgotten but cherished in the church.

Having been forgiven by God in Christ and having received the witness of the Holy Spirit, the drowtrodden came to know that they were the beloved of the Lord, gifted in many ways they hadn't imagined possible. Such graces created bonds of fellowship and care that transcended the divisions of class and hateful pride. Christian life offered the poor a different narrative through which they could come to know themselves in a new way, that is, as nothing less than the beloved of the Lord, as children of the Most High. –Kenneth J. Collins, *The Theology of John Wesley*

5. "ECCENTRIC FOOLS" LIKE JESUS CHRIST

Holiness people often have been thought of as believers belonging only to an earlier time. Their numerous "don'ts" supposedly were a damper on a well-rounded and joyous life. Men were stern and dominant; women were complacent and dressed very modestly. There's seemingly little in this dour picture but a cramped spiritual life that wouldn't attract modern people to the faith. But is there something from the holiness Christian movements of the past that's worthy of guiding Christian believers in the 21st century?

The true life of holiness refuses to accommodate claims of the Christian gospel to the debilitating effects of today's consumerist culture. Such social selfishness undermines faith in God and community with others by encouraging envy, greed, pride, and indulgence. Because of acceptance by God, holiness people are called to accept and treasure others. We are able to do this because our spiritual union with Christ compels us to move beyond ourselves toward others. We are inclined to give rather than always take. This counter-cultural kind of life is Christ's "eccentric" existence. It's to be mirrored in our eccentricity, our being "fools" like and for Christ. Eccentricity in the world's eyes was the very nature of Christ's presence with us and should be ours as well. –Don Thorsen and Barry L. Callen, *Heart & Life*

6. CHOOSE DOWNWARD MOBILITY

The Christian way is not upward mobility, the glitter of worldly success. It's the very opposite, choosing the path of pain, the way of *downward mobility*. It's the path of Jesus that ends on a self-sacrificing cross–which ironically turns out to be the very door to resurrection and eternal life. It's hard to release control and really serve God. There are many layers of self-justification rooted in personal ambition, goals, attitudes, and habits. These are wrong when they insist on serving the self-centered will. We face the temptation to reassert our control. Following Christ is not for the fainthearted.

Remember those great biblical prophets? They usually failed to get elected to anything other than the hall of shame. Often they were blunt in their presentations of the Word of God in order to get their harsh points across to deliberately deaf ears. Worship had gone very wrong among God's people. People were daring to smile at God and then do their own thing like God didn't exist (Isa. 29:13). When it's time to tell the truth, protecting one's reputation might be impossible. In the big picture, that really doesn't matter. –Kevin W. Mannoia, *The Integrity Factor*

7. NO PERIOD AFTER "I AM SAVED"

Here's a little lesson in Christian punctuation marks. A Christian should be careful about saying "I am saved." The problem is the period, not the testimony. The nature of our human situation does not permit many period-like punctuations. It's better to say, "I am saved," following the testimony with a *comma.* That unfinishedness is the reality that there still is the need to grow up into the full stature of Christ. We all are disciples still in the making, and God will be faithful to finish the task (Phil. 1:6). The period after that sentence is appropriate, although usually periods are a subtle form of arrogance and the seeds of spiritual stagnation. Few subjects in faith's grammar deserve an exclamation mark. Here's one. "Jesus is Risen!"

The theological point about commas is that we should be most careful not to claim that what is ongoing is really finished. We tend to say, "It happened and is over (period)" when the thing is still in process. We are "saved" from sin by God's sheer grace (comma or period?). Because the salvation issue is never fully done while we live in this world, we should opt for the comma. Of course, God's saving work has been fully done in the life, death, and resurrection of Jesus (! and .), but we sinners saved by grace are still in the salvation process (,). –Barry L. Callen, *Approaching Theology* and *Caught Between Truths*

8. THE GREAT EQUALIZER

We are drawn naturally to where we focus our eyes. Do you focus on the perimeters, defining Christian living in terms of the boundaries of theological doctrine, political persuasion, behavioral compliance, or social adherence? Doing so tends to result in a fear-based life that seeks to stay away from the limits lest you find yourself outside the approval of the faithful. Or do you focus on the center, staying close to the heart of the faith, relationship with the person of Jesus Christ? Doing so brings freedom to reach, live, flourish, dare, and not in fear of crossing a line but in hope of finding the fullness of life in pursuit of God.

Christian living is vibrant living, excited existence in motion toward the loving imagination of all that God has waiting for us. There is one level place in God's Kingdom where we all stand before the cross of Jesus without shoes. None are taller there than others. On this level ground, we all have equal access to hope and justice and an eternal future. Here we all are recipients of love and each has equal access to salvation through Jesus. The Kingdom is the great equalizer. Focus your eyes there! –Kevin W. Mannoia, *Church 2K*

9. QUESTIONS ARE VERY APPROPRIATE

The question mark suggests a level of still not knowing. Christians who capitalize on exclamation points and tend to use numerous periods where commas belong usually run scared of question marks. They insist, "We are to preach the truth, not dialogue about it as though it's up for grabs!" But what's wrong with humility and doubt? A mature person has little fear of being self-critical, and doubt can be a valuable means of clarification. It has a way of exposing false securities and even idolatrous views. To realize the possibilities of honest doubt is to be freed to plunge more deeply into an honest faith.

Explains Thomas Oden, "My life story has had two phases, going away from home as far as I could and then at last inhabiting my own original home of classic Christian wisdom." Theology deals with the largest questions of human origin, identity, and destiny. Gaining perspective on all this is a matter of faith as well as knowledge. Our knowledge will always have limitations. One can know and still not know. We must move beyond feeling guilty for sometimes doubting our faith. Indeed, there may be more genuine faith in honest doubt than in a blind acceptance of some conventional creed thoughtlessly held. Bring your questions off the bench and into the game. God can take it! –Barry L. Callen, *Approaching Theology*

10. GOD'S RESURRECTION POWER

Negative stereotypes have gathered around "holiness" and "Pentecostal" Christians. Follow the "method" and get the assured result, instant sanctification or a desired spiritual gift. Practice mouth and voice training and you will get the gift of tongues. Just come and it will be done. The stereotypes are many and not always unfounded. But holiness is not primarily the result of our efforts, our discipline and faithfulness, not the sure result of any set formula. Pride and arrogance over our spiritual achievements or superior gifts are always inappropriate. Christian life flows from divine grace and is not measured by human works.

We know that every good gift comes from above (Jam. 1: 17). The Apostle Paul tied heart renewal directly to the resurrection of Jesus. Paul's heart passion was, "I want to know Christ and the power of his resurrection" (Phil. 3:10). The resurrection of Jesus is something no human being can make happen by any effort. It rests solely on the power and amazing love of God. Therefore, since we know that all is from God, we are to walk humbly before the Lord, showing the true beauty of holiness and gladly employing whatever gifts we receive for the good of all. –Hubert P. Harriman and Barry L. Callen, *Color Me Holy*

11. WHAT IS AUTHENTIC RELIGION?

The Hebrew heritage of Christianity makes clear that authentic religion is far more than a code of conduct or even an "orthodox" creed. True faith must involve how a person walks daily in light of proper belief and in relationship with the ever-present God. Those who please God act justly, love mercy, and walk humbly with God

(Micah 6:8). The religious folks known by the prophet Amos were satisfied with their church services and at the same time cheating the poor in the streets. What does God really want? Shouted Amos to those "religious" folks, "Take away from me the noise of your songs; I will not listen to the melody of your hearts. But let justice roll down like waters and righteousness like an ever-flowing stream" (5:23–24).

Desert dwellers knew well the characteristics of a wadi, the stream bed. Much of the year it's broad and bone dry. When the rains come, however, the first rushing wall of water flows with such force that everything is swept away. Amos calls for justice to roll down like such a raging torrent, cleansing all evil before it and bringing new life to the desert. The fulcrum of social justice is Matthew 22:37-40. We are to love the Lord our God with everything we have and our neighbor as much as ourselves. –Richard Foster, *Streams of Living Water*

12. EMBRACING THE SCANDAL

Those of us from the Holiness and Pentecostal traditions often are given the dubious distinction of being the "embarrassing relatives" in the more centrist "evangelical clan." It's time to offer our own testimony without apology. Our "postmodern" time provides an ideal setting. It's intellectually respectable now to "let go and let God." I don't suggest bazaar demonstrations of the Holy Spirit, extremes that are genuine causes for concern. Here's a simple and maybe embarrassing fact. There may be an unclassifiable free speech that sometimes comes in response to the unclassifiable free God. In the face of God, standard human language can break down. There are gaps too large for such language to bridge, elements of spiritual life too deep for our usual words.

Let's dare to embrace without apology the "scandal" that some of us believers supposedly are. Those of us in the broad Wesleyan-Holiness-Pentecostal tradition of Christianity need to boldly pursue the quest for love's knowledge and love's language. We are known as a people of experiential religion. A core part of our tradition is a passion for God. Love is the unifying force and life-giving energy of the Christian life. In an important sense, all knowledge is relational.

Let's embrace each other as together we seek to embrace the unspeakable God. –Cheryl Bridges Johns, in the *Wesleyan Theological Journal* (1999)

13. YOU AREN'T STUCK IN THE MIDDLE!

The writer of the biblical book of Ecclesiastes is tempted to think that life in this world is little more than dust helplessly blowing away in the wind. If that's so, the best we can do is live for the moment and enjoy what little we can. We must come to terms with life as it really is, fickle, fragile, frustrating, and yet yielding at least flickers of hope. Even so, I think of the little-noticed fact about this biblical book if Ecclesiastes is placed between the psalms of David and the prophecies of Isaiah. Did the rabbis do this deliberately?

When really down, maybe we are being called to look in both directions. Look *back* and hear the singing of the grateful Hebrews finally freed from bondage (Ps.19:1-4). Then look *forward* to hear Isaiah's grand announcement that the people of God are about to be set free to go home because the future suddenly will open to them (Isa. 60:4-5). Even when caught in the middle of apparent negatives, we must be aware that we are surrounded by past goodness and being offered future hope! –Barry L. Callen, *Bible Stories for Strong Stomachs*

14. THE CENTRAL HALL OF LOVE

"Love" may be the most used and abused word in the English language. For so many, love is the high-sounding way of meeting my own needs, me-oriented instead of other-oriented. This serious misdirection has even seeped into the Christian faith. If I love God enough, God will bless me richly, maybe even with worldly goods. Love God and succeed in the business world and my bodily afflictions will evaporate. But true love is evidenced by what we *give away*, not by what *we get*. God so loved the world that he *gave* his only Son (Jn. 3:16). Christian "success" involves self-sacrifice. That announcement doesn't draw crowds, I realize. It's just the truth. Jesus said that an adequate fulfilling of the law will always be practicing the *law of love*.

Love takes the harshness out of holiness, the incredibility out of perfection, the moralism out of obedience, and the abstraction out of truth. John Wesley's whole approach to theology was built around the central theme of love to God and others. His thought is like a great rotunda with archway entrances all around. No matter which is entered, it always leads to the central Hall of Love. Looking upward toward the dome, one gazes into the inviting sky since there is no ceiling to love. It serves to link every doctrine together into one beautiful dynamic. –Mildred Bangs Wynkoop, *A Theology of Love*

15. LATHER YOUR MEMORIES WITH LOVE

The Lord's Prayer does not say that we are to forget what we have forgiven. It's our Father who is the great forgetter (Jer. 31:34). Paul says that love "keeps no record of wrongs" (1 Cor. 13:5). So are Christian disciples to have amnesia? For us humans, forgetting is hardly possible and in some ways not even desirable. To not forgive others is a serious error that jeopardizes our own forgiveness by God. But failing to remember what we have forgiven is full of significant danger as we pursue our spiritual journey. What Paul surely had in mind was something more like this. "Do not keep a record of the wrongs you have forgiven so that you can find ways *to get even over time.*"

A good memory is essential to spiritual growth, although using such memory for punitive purposes is to fall from God's grace and back into our own stage of being unforgiven by God. Quality memories guided by grace and lathered with love provide our strongest future. Learn from past wrongs, but only to build a wiser and more positive future. If there is any judgment deserved, leave that to God. –Barry L. Callen, *The Prayer of Holiness-Hungry People*

16. LOWER THE CENTER OF GRAVITY

Quality leadership formation honors the dynamic between the unseen identity at the bottom of the iceberg and the visible activity at its top. When leaders give regular attention to their core identity, their center of gravity remains solidly below the waterline. That's the source of their confidence and stability when circumstances around them are pushing and testing. A leader with a low center of gravity is able to meet performance expectations with proper perspective. That means putting on the mind of Christ. Before focusing on improvement of our behavior, we need replacement of our nature. Changed nature leads to changed behavior.

It's our responsibility to pursue a balance between identity and activity. Too often we evaluate leaders or ourselves by the success of our activities, how many people we've pleased, but such a limited perspective affirms the false assumption that effective leaders or mature spiritual life always manages to perform as desired and please people. That's judging only by the top of the iceberg. This is a trap that becomes performance-based identity where we define who we are, or who they are, only by what we or they do and how pleased we or they are. Instead, we are to be servants *of God*. –Kevin W. Mannoia, *The Integrity Factor*

17. WATCH OUT FOR THE EXHAUST!

City folks often don't do well on rural camping trips. It's the same when academic theologians appear in the world of ordinary Christians. The air can get a little chilly. Such a cultural clash was seen in Pennsylvania Amish country when a visiting family in their big car caught up to an Amish buggy. It was being pulled by a tired-looking horse. There was a hand-painted sign on the back of the buggy. "Energy Efficient Vehicle. Runs on Oats and Grass. Caution--Don't Step in the Exhaust!"

The seven deadly sins named by the Roman Catholic Church are pride, lust, greed, envy, sloth, wrath, and gluttony. These are bad but all personal. Shouldn't we be equally concerned to avoid stepping in those named by the Indian spiritual leader Mahatma Gandhi? He warned against politics without principle, wealth without work, commerce without morality, pleasure without conscience, education without character, science without humanity, and worship without sacrifice. Do you recognize any of these operating where you are? Is there a particular circumstance where you could reverse one of these negatives, even a little? Be careful what exhaust you are stepping in. Even tired-looking horses still have considerable capabilities!
–Barry L. Callen, *Approaching Theology*

18. THE WAY TO APPROACH LIFE

The university president I served offered this advice to graduates at the 1983 Commencement ceremony: "Be bold in your plans, modest in your self-esteem, unswerving in your dedication to Christ and his kingdom, and honorable in all your relationships. Be an open, redemptive, and loving human being. Keep the critical mind but not the critical spirit. Don't sit on the bank. Get in the swim of things. Never wallow in mediocrity. Try hard things for that's where the fun is. Try to stay green for that's where the growing happens." I want you to be that kind of graduate!

Resurrection is a big subject in the New Testament. It has to do with more than restoring life after bodies are dead. Resurrection is supposed to be a very present as well as an ongoing spiritual reality. We are to practice our death by giving up our will to live on our own terms. With such renunciation are we able to practice Christian resurrection. Renunciation death leads to resurrection life. "Eternal" life is being a reflector of God's own life being extended toward us and then going forth by our life's new ways. Eternal life a gift with no geographic boundaries or time restrictions. –Barry L. Callen, *The Living Dead*

19. IS RELIGION ALWAYS ESCAPIST?

Religion escapist? The answer is often yes, but sometimes no. Karl Marx was wrong in many ways, although sadly right that religion too often does function in escapist ways. It's that way when it denies the prevalence of pain in the world, avoids responsibility for the evil by assuming that God will take care of everything on his own, and explains evil as little more that the deserved divine judgment on the sins of other people. Sometimes evil is denied altogether by stressing a cheap and shallow promise of some pie-in-the-sky dream.

Jesus did say that the truth would make us free (Jn. 8:31–32). What he meant was freedom from sin, from imprisonment within the narrow walls of our own unenlightened self-interest, and from enslavement to our own shabbiest instincts, deceits, and self-deceptions. Christian freedom is *for* responsibility, not *from* it. The best moments any of us can have as human beings are when it becomes possible to escape the squirrel cage of being *me* into the landscape of the *us*. Love your enemies rather than misleading them; own your sins rather than being blind to them; accept the grace of God that can release us to sacrificial service and real joy. –Frederick Buechner, *Beyond Words*

20. GOD'S BUSINESS DONE GOD'S WAY

Is God well served by our erecting more impressive church buildings? Are we people of Jesus clever enough to work with the aggressive capitalists of the world and manage to avoid doing God's work in the world's way? Solomon built a magnificent temple in Jerusalem as a house for God. Supposedly wise or not, read 1 Kings 5 and 9 closely. David's son got hacked and he hacked back. Hiram, King of Tyre, was big in the lumber business and could cut quite a deal. Solomon got in the riddle business and cut back. Is this how temples and churches are to be built? God's people always have faced the daunting task of being special people in an ungodly world. We are to be and to do *as God is and does*. Solomon failed to always measure up, good reputation or not.

What is the intended role of the faithful church in relation to kings, presidents, giant corporations, even highly organized church denominations? Biblically speaking, it's clear that Christians are to be citizens of God's realm and rule (Phil. 3:20). Christ is the absolute head of the church, having first place in everything (Col. 1:13-18). There's a "Radical" tradition of Christianity calling for a "cleansing of the sanctuary," as Jesus once did in Jerusalem. Church compromises call for daring discipleship. How would Jesus go about his Father's work in today's world? –Barry L. Callen, *Bible Stories for Strong Stomachs,* and *Radical Christianity*

21. THERE'S A WIDENESS IN GOD'S MERCY

There is important middle ground in the tension between God as known definitively in Jesus and the potential salvation of the many persons not directly aware of God as Self-revealed through Jesus. Would God privilege only the properly informed and automatically damn all others (the majority of humans who have ever lived)? Biblical revelation reveals that, on the one hand, all salvation will be because of and *only* because of the message and merits of Jesus Christ. However, affirming the one God revealed in Jesus does not necessarily mean that God's saving grace is restricted to knowledge and acceptance of the specific Hebrew–Christian tradition. It does not mean that the unevangelized, those who have never heard, have no access to truly saving faith.

Does anyone experience God's freely offered salvation by a way other than Jesus Christ? No, Christ is the only way. Even so, God wishes salvation for all and intends to have mercy on all (1 Tim. 2:4; Rom. 11:32). God will save all who on the basis of the "light" they have respond to God in faith. It's faith in God that finally is crucial (Heb. 11:6), not necessarily hearing and consciously responding to the proclaimed gospel of Jesus Christ. There is an enlightening grace of God that goes before human evangelizing and to places evangelizing never reaches. It enables the Father God to be known in the Son by the ongoing and universal ministry of the Spirit of God. No one will be saved without Christ's atonement, but one need not be historically aware of that atonement in order to benefit from it.
–Clark H. Pinnock, *A Wideness in God's Mercy,* and John E. Sanders, in *Christian Scholar's Review* (1994)

22. I PLEDGE ALLEGIANCE

To sit at the Communion Table with Christ is to declare ultimate allegiance to Christ. It's joining the spiritual force that's working in this world to undermine and renew it. To be "holy" is to hold membership in a higher order than any human arrangement. It's to pledge allegiance to the King who is above all kings. At whatever cost, it's to be faithful to the new creation that Jesus Christ is bringing, one that soon will reign over all human kingdoms. Love one's country, yes. Love God's kingdom even more, absolutely! We are caught between contrasting biblical views of human governments. They are deserving of our obedience (Rom. 13) and sometimes revolting in God's eyes (Rev. 13). What we must never do is equate our loyalty to any nation with our loyalty to God!

Benjamin Franklin said: "He's a fool that makes his doctor his heir." Why foolishly tempt fate? We humans often act irrationally, tempting our own self-destruction. Passions of our bodies are allowed to hand disease the keys to our premature deaths. Our nationalisms reach the point of encouraging the world to arm itself with the capacity to annihilate the whole planet. Many defy the God who will be their eternal Judge. If only we were more conscious of the Great Physician and prepared to benefit from the glorious meanings of our opportunity to be God's heir, his loved and richly gifted children! –Barry L. Callen, *Catch Your Breath!* and *The Heart of the Matter*

23. WHAT CONTROLS CHRISTIAN FREEDOM?

A friend recounts the legalisms that stunted his early Christian life. Sin and going to the movies became the same thing when his parents "got religion." He suffered a stigma among his high school buddies. He was the non-smoking, non-dinking, non-card-playing, non-dancing kid from the strange church. Faith meant that he was stunted in life with many "don'ts." Authentic Christian discipleship requires both right beliefs and proper behaviors, of course. But who decides what are the proper behaviors, and are there so many negatives that all joy is drained from our existence? Jesus decided that the "traditions of the Elders" were no longer the absolute safeguards against sin and the misuse of freedom. What is?

Paul responds, "The Holy Spirit!" Live by the Spirit and don't gratify the desires of the flesh. There is one law, that *of love*. The whole law is summed up in a single commandment, "You shall love your neighbor as yourself" (Gal. 5:14). While God calls disciples to freedom, Paul announces a caution. "Do not use your freedom as an opportunity for self-indulgence" (Gal. 5:13b). Believers must know that Christian holiness is not primarily two common things. It's not *asceticism* (denying ourselves to death) or *athleticism* (working ourselves to death). Instead, it's *acceptance*, allowing God's Spirit to love us into new, abundant, and finally everlasting lives that do the right because we love the right. –Barry L. Callen, *Christian Holiness*

24. GIVE ATTENTION TO THE FATHERS *AND MOTHERS*

As Christian "feminists" explore Scripture, they critique some traditional biblical interpretations and construct new ones designed to liberate all people and revitalize a fuller understanding of God with us and in us all, male and female. They paint a picture of God's passionate pain-love. Like God, Christian feminists note carefully the experiences of the silenced, exploited, and oppressed. They give careful attention, for instance, to the Cappadocian Mothers as well as Fathers. The fathers are well known, Gregory Nazianzen, Basil, Gregory of Nyssa, etc. But who were the mothers?

They often were influencers behind their famous male counterparts. They were highly sensitive to the crucial subject of "deification," the realization of the image of God being restored within us fallen humans. How different modern Christianity might be if the Cappadocian deification process had become the Christian mainstream instead of Augustine, who emphasized Eve's role in the fall and the entrance of sin into the world. How different if these Cappadocian fathers and mothers had continued their family tree instead of living their unmarried ascetic and religious lives. Insight and power come from a combination of the masculine and feminine, mature thought and transformed life. –Karen Strand Winslow, *Imagining Equity*, and Carla D. Sunberg, *The Cappadocian Mothers*

25. TESTIMONY OF THE EMPOWERED HOLY LIFE

Readers of my *The Triumphs of His Grace* would understandably ask, "How do you account for the change from a 17-year-old boy escaping the confines of a radical holiness tabernacle to the presidency of three Christian institutions of higher learning and a leadership role in the world Wesleyan movement?" The gap is so great that my story teeters on the edge of disbelief. The answer roots in my conclusion as a teenager. "I left with my freedom as a flame and holiness as my thirst." My view of Wesleyan holiness changed from fractured perfectionism to holistic beauty.

My deepest desire came to share in John Wesley's vision of human wholeness. I want the whole Christ as my Savior, the whole

Bible as my guide, the whole Church as my fellowship, and the whole world as my mission field. My desired legacy? I want holiness, the indwelling Spirit, as my experience, with wholeness, personal and social, as its evidence. I want to be known as a role player in God's great redemptive drama, planting and watering seeds, with the growth exclusively given by God. And finally, I want to be found faithful to all who come behind me. –David L. McKenna, *Threads of His Grace*

26. PACK AND USE YOUR BUNGEE CORD

We Christians are to live in the tension of the left and right, always anchored in the middle. That's where the effects of a strong foundation and a robust mission are most felt and effective. To the doctrinal purest this tension represents pressure toward dangerous drift. To the missional activist, this tension resists any stodgy, irrelevant conservatism that refuses any motion. In the active middle is where Wesleyan-Holiness people should live and thrive. We are both profoundly conservative in our anchored identity and passionately active in our missional engagement. We are middle-way and on-the-move people.

This *via media* does not mean we are compromised in a muddled accommodation. It means that as we travel we always pack a bungee cord for exercise and wisdom development. We wrap its middle around the doorknob of our room, back away, and with each end in a hand we stretch it back and forth. We are anchored and stretching, believing even while exploring, going on without losing our roots, becoming stronger as we engage in the fray. We grow as we go.
–Kevin W. Mannoia, *Via Media*

Early let us seek Thy favor,
early let us do Thy will;
Blessed Lord, and only Savior,
with Thy love our bosoms fill . . . (Dorothy A. Thrupp)

By your blessed Word obeying, Lord, we prove
our love sincere; for we hear you gently saying,
"Love will do as well as hear" . . . (Daniel S. Warner)

No condemnation now I dread;
Jesus, and all in him, is mine!
Bold I approach the eternal throne, and
Claim the crown, through Christ, my own . . . (Charles Wesley)

Now make our fragile hearts,
both strong and brave,
and send us into a dying
world to save . . . (William Booth)

Would you be free from the burden of sin?
There's power in the blood, power in the blood.
Would you o'er evil of victory win?
There's wonderful power in the blood . . . (Lewis Edgar Jones)

Guide me, O Thou great Jehovah,
Pilgrim through this barren land;
I am weak, but Thou art mighty,
Hold me with Thy powerful hand . . . (William Williams)

Lead on, O King eternal, the day of march has come;
Henceforth in fields of conquest, Thy tents shall be our home.
Through days of preparation, Thy grace has made us strong,
And now, O King eternal, we lift our battle song . . .
(Ernest W. Shurtleff)

His yoke is easy, His burden is light,
I've found it so, I've found it so;
His service is my sweetest delight,
His blessings ever flow . . . (Daniel S. Warner)

Lord, dismiss us with Thy blessing,
Fill our hearts with joy and peace;
Let us each Thy love possessing,
Triumph in redeeming grace . . . (John Fawcett)

The Truths of God
For the People of God

About that day and hour no one knows, only the
Father. . . . Be alert at all times. . . . "All authority
in heaven and on earth has been given to me (Jesus).
Go therefore and make disciples of all nations."
(Matt. 24:36; Lk. 21:36; Matt. 28:18-19)

When this perishable body puts on imperishability,
then the saying that is written will be fulfilled: "Death
has been swallowed up in victory. Where, O death, is
your victory?" . . . "I am the Alpha and the Omega," says
the Lord God, who is, and who was, and who is to come,
the Almighty. (1 Cor. 15:54; Rev. 1:8)

VIII

The Hope that Genuinely Assures

The Apostles' Creed is an ancient and still a good Christian guide to matters of the end times and ultimate future. Little is yet known about the eventual tomorrows. What this creed presents is consensus Christian thinking from the earliest times which makes clear that what little is known is more than enough. Our present responsibilities as representatives of Jesus are crucial and not to be violated. Violation happens by useless waiting on the tomorrow that is sure to be or speculating imaginatively beyond what little currently is known about the distant tomorrows.

Here's what the creed assures us is known about the coming future and how it's to relate to discipleship today. The right will prevail. Jesus is now resurrected and always holds tomorrow in his hands. Life will win! We are to be thrilled by God's promised future without being paralyzed by the anticipation of an arriving paradise. There's mission now before the awards later. That's all we know now, and it's more than enough. Following are twenty-two golden nuggets of Christian expectation that seek to set wise guidelines about focusing on *then,* but only in ways that stimulate mission *now.*

Glimpses of the following Golden Nuggets

1. God's love will never pass away, even if all else does.
2. The Spirit of God already has come, so act alive now!
3. In a sense, we begin at the end. Then can and should be now.

4. Walk toward the waiting lions wrapped in a sacred song.
5. Don't distract the church with any clever predictive theories.
6. Don't look for the detail of today's news in ancient prophecy.
7. A case study of the wrong predictive direction.
8. The Book of Revelation can be freshly understood.
9. Embody in the present the relevance of our future hope.
10. The resurrected Jesus opens a new future.
11. What happens after the sun goes cold?
12. Our souls should grow deep like the rivers.
13. If the grave of Jesus is empty, death itself has died!
14. An Open Door to Home.
15. An eternal sunrise is certain!
16. When will the end be? Soon, beginning now!
17. God is spiritual spring, seed of a new tomorrow.
18. The goal is a grand vision of the church, not just of me.
19. Who gets crushed under the chariot wheels of time?
20. The church is the place to focus our telescopes.
21. Polycarp was martyred, but Jesus Christ lives forever!
22. We know at least this—the end is only the beginning.

1. ANTICIPATIONS OF HEAVEN BELOW

John Wesley said it well. "Whosoever will reign with Christ in heaven must have Christ reigning with him on earth." Grace and love are central to Wesleyan identity and remain central to the Holiness and Pentecostal movements of Christianity that have followed. Their's is an optimism of grace, an expectancy that through the power of the Holy Spirit God can and does transform lives, renew churches, and reform societies in ways that more faithfully mirror the life of the coming Kingdom. The key word to describe this "eschatological" life is *love*, revealed most fully in the life, death, and resurrection of Jesus Christ for the redemption of the whole world.

While all else may pass away, love never will. The crucified Jesus is risen and coming again. When the kingdom of heaven is fully established, God's love will reign supreme. But it reigns even now in human hearts and lives and communities that feature the love of Christ in their worship and ministries, and wherever it's expressed through acts of compassion and cries for justice. This love is a present working reality as well as a future hope. It's an active anticipation of heaven below. –Henry H. Knight III, *Anticipating Heaven Below*

2. PREFER TO BE DEAD?

Here's the recollection of a perceptive poet of life. He was driving on a country road when suddenly he spotted a man along the road carrying an enormous scythe on his shoulder. As he flew past, the driver turned and their glances met. Voltage ran through the driver. There was nothing to do but keep driving, turn off the radio, and start noticing how white the houses were, how red the barns and green the sloping fields. Just glimpsing death makes life appear so sweet and precious. Spotting the end can bring new beginnings that allow the present to move more wisely into the future. If the unexamined life is not worth living, why do most of us act like we prefer to be dead?

Being "holy" is less a perfect waiting for the Lord's return and more a perfect loving and active serving in the meantime. We all have unanswered questions about the end times. Such questions must not render us passive believers just waiting and aimlessly driving down the road. Sitting out the present, waiting for the perfect set of circumstances, is an intolerable and unholy stance. Christian holiness is *love in action now*. God's promises are sure. While Jesus will return, his Spirit *already has come*. Therefore, what's clear is the call to go on God's mission now! True saints don't sit and wait but are filled with the already-present Spirit who goes and serves. The harvest fields are ripe and waiting for our harvest. –Barry L. Callen, *All of God's Word for All of My Needs* and *God in the Shadows*

3. WHO CAN AND SHOULD WE BE NOW?

Jesus' resurrection promises that the God who loves the world will neither abandon his people nor ignore their corruption. The divine plan is to redeem what is corruptible as part of an overall renewal of the creation. Thus, Christian believers should prayerfully seek purification in eager expectation of embracing the Lord Jesus upon his return. The critical matter for now concerns how eternity's beckoning cuts into each present moment of existence. The Spirit's calling from heaven can be seen as intersecting each instant of the space-time continuum.

Every breath is an opportunity to shape an eternal path. In a sense we begin at the end because human beings live ultimately for what they hope for, what they desire, what they love. This is true even as we still perceive all through a mirror dimly. It's the Holy Spirit who makes present and real the resurrected and living Christ. Scripture remains normative, even if its meaning and application allow for a number of interpretations and applications through which the Spirit communicates the personal truth that Jesus Christ is always with us. –Amos Yong, *Renewing Christian Theology*

4. HE'S ALREADY COME!

Too many Christians spend their time speculating about when Jesus will come again. They miss something of fundamental importance that enables holy lives in the meantime. Jesus *already has come*! At Pentecost the Spirit of Christ came *to* us in order to be *in* us (experienced holiness) so that God may move *through* us as love to a broken world (expressed holiness). Let's avoid future speculation and focus on present proclamation. Jesus being here now makes all the difference in what may yet be prior to the end of all things.

Recall Jesus in that Upper Room with enemies already lurking just outside the door. He shared a sacred time of encouragement with his disciples and then, when they had sung a hymn, went out. His departure was covered with memory, defiance, and doxology. He walked toward the waiting lions wrapped in a sacred song of his community's faith. Fresh notes of memory and rhythms of hope radiated through his very being. The people of Jesus can be in deep trouble and at the same time pulsate with a vibrant rejoicing. Pain can be managed by pairing it with remembering and rejoicing.
–Barry L. Callen, *Catch Your Breath!* and *The Jagged Journey*

5. POLITICAL INTERPRETATIONS OF END TIMES?

Approaches to interpreting the Bible's references to the ultimate future often try to force Jesus' second coming. Force it? Yes, there are efforts by some to promote and even hasten the fulfillment of biblical prophecies that they believe must first come to pass before the return. Some believe that first the modern nation of Israel needs to recapture Arab lands, rebuild the temple in Jerusalem, and so on. To ensure a fulfillment of these presumed prophecies, they sometimes promote violence, war, and other atrocities in God's name. Sometimes known as "Zionism," Jewish and Christian, there is support for Israel "right or wrong" without subjecting actions to normal Christian ethical analysis.

Such rash interpreters of biblical "prophecy" obsess over conspiracy theories having to do with a "one world order" or engage in speculations about who might be the "Antichrist." They muse over whether a news report this morning likely is the fulfillment of some verse in Daniel or Revelation and send money to preachers who claim they know for sure. Lamentably, some Protestants have accused Roman Catholic popes of being the Antichrist, and more recently have tended to accuse certain U. S. presidents (usually of the opposing political party) of being the Antichrist. In fact, Christians ought to be wary about such dangerous thinking and acting that may be motivated more by power politics, economics, and nationalism than biblical revelation. –Don Thorsen, *What's True about Christianity?*

6. THE TEMPTATION TO MORBID CURIOSITY

End times speculation can only create divisions in the Body of Christ and distract from church mission. The reality of Christ, his second advent, the consummation of the kingdom, and the eternal abode of the saints are precious truths of the faith and firmly grounded in the Word of God. They should not be aborted by future speculations that seek to pry into mysteries that transcend our present state of knowledge. We must stop constructing clever systems that claim to depict history in advance. That's been done many times across church history and now shown to have been misguided and costly.

No speculation should become a preoccupation that diverts from preaching the good news that God has *already* decisively won the victory over sin and Satan in this present age. God can deliver from all sin *here and now*. No flaunting of our morbid curiosities about tomorrow should take away from a stimulus to holiness today. Such flaunting, even if well-intentioned, is unacceptable and hurtful to the church and its intended unity. We must not to be dogmatic about tomorrow's speculative matters when God's mission today remains very unfinished. –H. Ray Dunning, *Grace, Faith & Holiness*

7. A CASE STUDY IN FAILED END-TIME SPECULATION

Hal Lindsey was a Christian Zionist, dispensational premillennialist, and fundamentalist. These adjectives suggest a Christian man of strong conviction rooted in a series of clear pre-judgments about what truth should be and how it's to be interpreted. On the heels of the Six-Day War (1967) when Israel captured key territory from its Arab neighbors, he wrote his best-selling book of biblical prophecy (*The Late, Great Planet Earth*). It identifies the modern State of Israel as key to present biblical fulfillment. Hal says this book was popular because he had quit listening to the Bible "scholars" and finally had let the biblical prophets speak for themselves. What he doesn't say is that he would be revising his interpretation as new developments would come along in years to follow, and that all interpretations of this kind across Christian history have proven wrong.

This irony of certainty and yet wrongness fits dozens of Lindseys across the centuries. It argues convincingly that such an approach to biblical interpretation is faulty, mere human speculation. The many buyers of Lindsey's book loved his sense of certainty and drama playing out in the morning news. But he was a victim of wrong assumptions about the nature and intent of the Bible's prophetic material. What grabs wide attention doesn't determine Bible teaching. Lindsey's book is as fanciful as fascinating. The Bible does not provide calendars and grand political schemes with contemporary nametags. Its "apocalyptic" literature needs understood for what it is, not for what excites us. –Barry L. Callen, *The Heart of the Matter*

8. THE BOOK OF REVELATION, THEN AND NOW

The message of the Book of Revelation was first directed to a situation of persecution that was threatening the Christian church with demands for emperor worship. That historical setting doesn't provide detailed clarity about the ultimate end of the age. If the initial application of the final biblical book, the problem of emperor worship in the first century, exhausted the meaning of this revelation, it would have only limited interest to us now. However, its application is not limited to that time. This book continues to have great significance as continuing divine revelation.

The fact that the dynamics of one historical event foreshadow the final struggle becomes the basis for the possibility of a fresh prophetic understanding in every age. John's prophecy can relate to situations in subsequent times that are illuminated by his visions. This relation does not allow us to make a one-to-one correlation between the original prophecy and any historical crisis after the original one. Any contemporary application always must be grounded in the past, which then sheds light on the present rather than providing specific predictions of present particulars. –H. Ray Dunning, *Biblical Heights for Today's Valleys*

9. GOD'S TIMING IS NOW!

A focus on God's future should not be a matter of mere curiosity for Christians, but a foundation on which responsible discipleship rests. Too often what is crucial is allowed to become an obstacle to the very thing it's meant to support. The timing most crucial for Christians isn't "When will Jesus return?" but "What does his sure return require of believers in the meantime?" God's time is *now*! The pressing issue is not speculating on details of God's coming future but addressing how best to relate "final things" and "present responsibilities." How should the *then* of faith's expectations relate to the intended *now* of faith's mission?

The Christian community was launched initially by vigorous preaching about the bursting forth of a New Age in the "last days." The first Christian evangelists were sure they knew what time it was in God's eyes. It was the fullness of time, the beginning of the end, the present arrival of the Kingdom in the coming of Jesus. A central concern is to avoid distracting speculation about details of the future and focus instead on the intended faithfulness of God's people *in the meantime*, embodying in the present the relevance of our hope for the future. The burden of the New Testament message clearly is the call for the church to be on mission *now*. –Barry L. Callen, *Faithful in the Meantime*

10. IT TOOK THE RESURRECTION

Listen to this paraphrase of Rabbi Jesus. I realize that seeing me on the cross was devastating to your faith. It was an inevitable question. How could the true Messiah be so humiliated by this world? It would take my resurrection for you to realize that what you saw on the cross was not the triumph of this world's power. It was an unexpected presentation of the amazing power of the love of my Father for all of lost humankind. That awful death of mine was completely voluntary and totally for you and a picture of who my Father really is. When all else is gone, that sacrificial love will stand for all eternity. Receive God's gift and be that holy love yourselves, holy light in action in your time.

We who believe don't know many of the whats, whens, and hows related to the final resolution of life's big questions about tomorrow and eternity. By faith, however, we do know *Who*. The future finally will be shaped by and in the full control of Rabbi Jesus, the One who already has come and is well known to us. The best faith-abiding, therefore, is the posture of *Christ-celebrating*. Be sure of *Who* and the whats, whens, and hows of tomorrow will take care of themselves. –Barry L. Callen, with Steve Hoskins, *A Year with Rabbi Jesus*

11. BEYOND THE "BIG BANG"

"Eschatology" (end-times study) has a fresh place among Christian theologians dialoguing with modern scientists. The "Big Bang" paradigm of beginnings assumes that the universe is walking a one-way street from hot to cold. The sun eventually will burn out. There will be an inevitable conclusion to the universe. It's on a straight arrow toward total destruction. Added now is the additional potential of planetary suicide either by nuclear war or ecological asphyxiation because of us humans. Secularists see in this no moral dimension. It's just how things are. They could be right, or quite blind.

Not so with the writer of the biblical book of Hebrews. "In the beginning, O Lord, you laid the foundations of the earth and the heavens are the work of your hands. They will perish, but you remain. They will all wear out like a garment. You will roll them up like a robe; like a garment they will be changed. But you remain the same, and your years will never end" (Heb. 1:10–12). There also is the New Testament echo of Isaiah's prophecy of "a new heaven and new earth" in which righteousness dwells (2 Pet. 3:13, Rev. 21:1–5). Christian "end times" belief involves the promise of a new reality from the eternal God who makes all things new. God is not threatened by the apparent inevitability of a winding down of this present order. God is skilled at rewinding as he chooses. –Michael Lodahl, *Wesleyan Theological Journal* (1994)

12. DEEP LIKE THE RIVERS

Langston Hughes had never written a poem when he was in the eighth grade and elected the class poet. He surmised the election was because he was African-American and Whites thought "all Negroes can sing and dance and have a sense of rhythm." In the following decades Hughes would write 16 books, 20 plays, 10 collections of short stories, and many essays, radio scripts, and song lyrics. The inscription above his buried ashes in Harlem are words from his great poem "The Negro Speaks of Rivers." It reads, "My soul has grown deep like the rivers."

When the end of life comes, I want to have lived not only its full length, but also its width, height, and depth. How about you? Here's really good news. There is divine help for the journey! God not only gives bread from heaven and water from the rock but the needed resources to survive the journey through life and complete it even to eternity. –Barry L. Callen, *God in the Shadows*

13. DEATH HAS DIED!

If the story of the resurrected Jesus is the record of an hallucination or optical illusion, or if it's only the fabrication of the overworked imaginations of a few unlettered disciples, then the Christian movement has been a mere exercise in misleading stupidity. However, if Jesus did die and then live again, and no evidence to the contrary has ever been produced, then his resurrection is the most important thing that has ever happened on the human scene. If his grave was empty then, it still is. Death has died! Can you hear Jesus saying even now, "Because I live, you can live also." The New Testament teaching about the "resurrection of the body" means at least that in the life beyond you will still be you and I will still be me. How we then will be packaged doesn't matter and is beyond our knowing.

Cheryl Bridges Johns has made clear what we should do. "I appeal to those in the Wesleyan-Holiness and Pentecostal traditions to embrace the heart of both of our movements, namely, the quest for *love's knowledge*. John Wesley understood love as the unifying force and life-giving energy of the Christian life. It's a knowing which is not a grasping but a letting go, a knowing that is not grounded in its own self-presence but in the presence of the source of all knowledge. Love's knowledge is *relational*." –Barry L. Callen, with Steve Hoskins, *A Year with Rabbi Jesus*

14. AN OPEN DOOR TO HOME

Death is the moment of our return to God. It's the end of the journey, the culmination of our "yes" response to God. It's the opening of the eternal life we've already begun to live in union with Christ. Death is not defeat, then, but the moment of fulfillment. God calls us to our final rest, which is in God's own everlasting embrace. Through the Spirit we wait for the hope of righteousness (Gal. 5:5) when the Spirit brings creation home to its Maker.

God is with us. Therefore, let us live in God's presence and bathe in his love. Let us grow into union with God, yoked together with others in the faith community and eagerly awaiting the Marriage Supper of the Lamb. Eternity is within our hearts, pressing upon our time-torn lives, warming us with intimations of an astounding destiny, calling us home unto itself. "My soul longs, indeed it faints for the courts of the Lord; my heart and my flesh sing for joy to the living God" (Ps. 84:1-2). –Clark H. Pinnock, *Flame of Love*

15. THE SUNRISE IS CERTAIN

If God truly is God, then one day, beyond the time when time as we know it is no more, whatever God intends will be. The sun of eternity will rise with shafts of forever-light bursting forth. While not quite yet, it's coming and it's unstoppable. Paul reassures the Philippians and all of us that the same God "who began a good work in you will carry it on to completion" (Phil.1:6). One day, all will be eternal light. What are we to do while the divine sunrise is delayed? According to Paul, "the night is about over, morning is about to break. Be up and awake to what God is doing! God is putting the finishing touches on the salvation work he began when we first believed" (Rom. 13:12).

Pilate once responded with super-pathetic words that still ring down the ages, causing a silly bit of laughter. He told his men to "make the tomb of Jesus as secure as you can." That instruction was like shouting "Stop!" to the rising sun or "No!" to the ocean's coming high tide. Poor Pilate. He was ordering his men to barricade the tomb of God! The body of Jesus was destined to resurrection no matter what mere humans said or did. The dawning of the Light of the world was completely inevitable. It still is. –Barry L. Callen, *God in the Shadows* and *The Jagged Journey*

16. ONE DAY SOON—AND EVEN NOW

True Christian believers have learned history's real direction. One day, someday soon, there will come the culmination of all time and space. With Jesus Christ always the center of history's meaning and hope and the future's certainty, his Father stands steady and supreme. The grand story of redemption stretching across millennia eventually will be brought to an end. God once declared through Isaiah: "Behold, I will create new heavens and a new earth" (65:17). This promise became the basis of the following vision recorded in the Book of Revelation: "Then I saw a new heaven and new earth, for the first heaven and the first earth had passed away" (21:1).

Grace, love, and therefore optimism have been central to the very identity of the Wesleyan, Holiness, and Pentecostal movements. There is an expectancy that, through the power of the Holy Spirit, God does transform lives, renew churches, and reform society in ways that more faithfully mirror the life of the coming Kingdom. All else may pass away, but love never will because the crucified Jesus is risen and indeed coming again. In fact, the coming Kingdom of love already is established in the hearts and lives and communities of those who now mirror the love of Christ through acts of compassion and cries for justice. –Henry H. Knight III, *Anticipating Heaven Below*

17. LIFE WINS!

The best days for the church still lie ahead. Read it almost anywhere in the Bible. Start with Isaiah, Daniel, or Revelation. Troubles there surely were then but hope was already seen bursting over the horizon. The pattern of the past is that every reverse is followed by a fresh step forward. Keep marching whatever the enemy fire! Paul points to the final conclusion. "Then comes the end when Christ hands over the kingdom to God the Father after he has destroyed every ruler and authority and power. For he must reign until he has put all enemies under his feet" (1 Cor. 15:24-25). Discouraged? Look up and move on!

Believers can sing with joy because God is, God has, and one day God will do all necessary for our well-being. This is the keynote of the biblical psalms and the bedrock of Christian faith. Whatever happens, all is secure. God is the spiritual springtime who is our shield for today and the seed of our better tomorrow. Praise God that the morning light is sure to come! Live today as the Lord directs and do not be disabled by constant wars and rumors of wars. Whatever is happening or yet will come, it will pass. God remains forever!
–Barry L. Callen, *All of God's Word for All of My Needs*

18. IT'S NOT ALL ABOUT *ME*

The Judeo-Christian tradition features a corporate mentality. God promised Abraham a people and promised a land for that people. We now live in the Western world that's much more individualistic in mind-set. When will the end come, and how, and then what about *me*, heaven, hell, maybe something in between? In response to such questions, Jesus offered at least this. Don't worry, be faithful, all will be well. The task of believers is to focus now on bringing to reality the current presence of God's coming community. The church of God should be our present preoccupation, as well as future expectation.

Biblical "prophecy" speaks of the goal of history being the glorious reign of God in a corporate setting of reconciliation and fellowship. Inhabitants then will live in harmony with each other, with creation, and with God in one glorious community. It will be a new corporate order, a new Jerusalem (Rev. 21:9–21). The intended goal of our human story is one new humanity in Christ (Eph. 2:15), the fellowship of those whom Christ purchased for God "from every tribe and language and people and nation" (Rev. 5:9). Through the work of the Spirit, the seeds of that eventual fellowship are being planted even now. –Stanley J. Grenz, *Theology for the Community of God*

19. THE CHARIOT WHEELS OF TIME

With all the coming and going, all the being born and dying, there's built into the creation a reason and rhythm that comes from beyond the merely human sphere. It's grace-full and seeking to pull us toward our life beyond all death. We tend to focus on the many deaths among the fragile living whom we know. We are so aware of much grief across our years. We must learn to shift our focus to the life beyond death, finding the joy that overcomes grief, seeing the hope that seeks our attention.

That's the bigger picture that can make all the difference now as well as later. Why the excitement? "For the Lord our God Almighty reigns!" (Rev. 19:6). Here's the central fact known by Jesus and rarely known by others. Pilate, Herod, and Caesar all were little more than dust beneath the chariot wheels of time. Jesus was helpless in their hands, or so they thought. Now they are mere memories of a distant yesterday while he is the hope of today and the heaven that will be tomorrow. *Hallelujah!* –Barry L. Callen, *The Living Dead*

20. SEEING THROUGH KINGDOM EYES

Opening a portal of hope is perhaps the most important contribution that can be made for the person who is depressed, lost, or dying. The hope of the Kingdom of God gives the bigger perspective on life, one not limited by our physical beings. Seeing with Kingdom eyes clarifies that life is never terminal. Church life should be a hope-producing garden of grace. This hopeful vision is given by God, not developed by people or pastors. Even so, the community of faith is to be guided by and sharing the heavenly vision of the best that's yet ahead.

Together, the people of God are to come to know themselves as looking at the moon of divine destiny through the telescope of God's revelation. The people of God are the saints who refract the light to bring it close. The pastor serves to point the telescope and serve as the eyepiece bringing it into focus. Pastors and people don't create

God's vision but enable its clearer perception. That is the hopeful nature of the body of Christ at work in advancing the work of God. The Spirit in the church serves to enable the people to view life and the future through Kingdom eyes. –Kevin W. Mannoia, *15 Characteristics of Effective Pastors*

21. GREAT LAST TESTIMONIES

My first teacher of Christian theology shared a little testimony with me when he was eighty years old. He called himself a "progressive evangelical." Most important to him theologically were only these things. God seemed closer than ever and Christ sweeter than ever. Being loyal to the kingdom of God was more important than ever. Beyond that, he said, "I'm not going to be picky or judging about anything. Playing God has never been appealing." What a better church and world this would be if we all shared his testimony!

Only a few years after the biblical book of Revelation was written, the old Polycarp faced martyrdom in Smyrna because of his unrelenting Christ-likeness and Christ-witness. He refused to deny his love for Christ, so they burned him alive. When the church recorded what happened, the glorious words were: "Polycarp was martyred, Statius Quadratus being proconsul of Asia, *and Jesus Christ being King forever!*" One was alive forever and the other dead only for the moment. That's worth a big "Amen!" and "Hallelujah!" –Barry L. Callen, *The Jagged Journey*

22. THE END IS THE BEGINNING

Hope can be the fool's paradise, and yet the future of eternal life is not so completely up in the air. I put forward three considerations. 1. The God of Abraham, Isaac, and Jacob is "the God of hope" for he promises life and keeps his promises. God's whole being is faithfulness. The acts of God in history open up the future, and all created life is life in its beginnings. 2. Jesus has been raised from the dead and become the Christ of the future. The New Testament calls him the first fruit of those who have fallen asleep and the leader of life. Through his raising from the dead, the all-embracing prospect of the life of the future world has been opened up for the living and the dead.

3. In the community of Christ we experience God's Spirit as a power of life which makes us live. This is an infectious livingness which shows itself in affirmed life and new courage for living. Because in this experience of life we come close to the eternal origin of all things, these powers of life are also powers of the future world. They are powers which come into our mortal life here from the eternal life on the other side of death, and they kindle the beginning of the life which reaches beyond death. –Jürgen Moltmann, *In the End—The Beginning*

God is our refuge and our strength,
in him our hope is found;
an ever-present help in need,
when trouble is around . . . (Timothy and Julie Tennent)

Unto the hills, I lift my eyes;
from whence shall come my aid?
My help is from the Lord alone,
who heaven and earth has made . . . (Psalm 121)

We have a Savior to show to the nations,
who the path of sorrow hath trod;
That all of the world's great peoples
might come to the truth of God . . . (H. Ernest Nichol)

When the trumpet of the Lord shall sound, and time shall be no more, when the saved of earth shall gather over on the other shore and the roll is called up yonder, I'll be there! . . . (James M. Black)

There's a land that is fairer than day,
and by faith we can see it afar,
for the Father waits over the way,
to prepare us a dwelling place there . . . (Sanford F. Bennett)

Soar, we now where Christ his led,
Following our exalted Head;
Made like him, like him we rise,
Ours the cross, the grave, the skies! . . . (Charles Wesley)

We're marching to Zion,
beautiful, beautiful Zion,
we're marching upward to Zion,
the beautiful city of God . . . (Isaac Watts)

Now I've a hope that will surely endure
after the passing of time;
I have a future in heaven for sure,
there in those mansions sublime . . . (John W. Peterson)

God be with you till we meet again;
Keep love's banner floating o'er you,
Smite death's threatening wave before you,
God be with you till we meet again . . . (Jeremiah E. Rankin)

Contributors

The following names are only those wise authors who have contributed text entries in this book. There are many other precious souls who contributed the hymn lyrics that give musical harmony and spiritual depth to theological narrative. "Objective" theology and Christian "experience" are never to be separated. Praise God for the communion of the saints!

William J. Abraham
George Barna
C. K. Barrett
Paul M. Bassett
David R. Bauer
Charles E. Blake
Cheryl Bridges Johns
Delwin Brown
Frederick Buechner
Barry L. Callen
Paul Chilcote
Daniel B. Clendenin
Winn Collier
Kenneth J. Collins
Curtiss Paul DeYoung
Kevin DeYoung
Donald W. Dayton
H. Ray Dunning
Thomas N. Finger
Richard J. Foster
Roger Green
Stanley J. Grenz

Shirley C. Guthrie, Jr.
Georgia E. Harkness
Hubert P. Harriman
Ivan L. Hartsfield
Stanley Hauerwas
D. Michael Henderson
Steve Hoskins
Langston Hughes
T. D. Jakes
E. Stanley Jones
Dennis F. Kinlaw
Henry H. Knight, III
Steven J. Land
Diane Leclerc
Michael Lodahl
David L. McKenna
Randy L. Maddox
Kevin W. Mannoia
V. James Mannoia, Jr.
James Earl Massey
Thomas Merton
T. Crichton Mitchell

Jürgen Moltmann
M. Robert Mulholland, Jr.
Henri J. Nouwen
Thomas C. Oden
Roger E. Olson
Eugene H. Peterson
Clark H. Pinnock
Jonathan A. Powers
Jonathan S. Raymond
Richard Rohr
John E. Sanders
Timothy L. Smith
Howard A. Snyder
Gilbert W. Stafford
James S. Stewart
Douglas M. Strong

Carla D. Sunberg
Don Thorsen
Robert A. Traina
David Elton Trueblood
Bernie A. Van De Walle
Jason Vickers
Arthur Wainwright
Keith Ward
Steve Wilkens
William Willimon
Karen Strand Winslow
Ben Witherington
Laurence W. Wood
Mildred Bangs Wynkoop
Amos Yong

www.ingramcontent.com/pod-product-compliance
Lightning Source LLC
Chambersburg PA
CBHW060624250426
43670CB00056B/2200